T3-BPF-999

JOSEPH BRANT
AND HIS WORLD

Eighteenth-Century Mohawk Warrior
and Statesman

JAMES W. PAXTON

James Lorimer & Company Ltd., Publishers
Toronto

Copyright © 2008 James W. Paxton

All rights reserved. No part of this book may be reproduced or transmitted in any form or by any means, electronic o mechanical, including photocopying, or by any information storage or retrieval system, without permission in writin from the publisher.

James Lorimer & Company Ltd., Publishers acknowledge the support of the Ontario Arts Council. We acknowledge th support of the Government of Canada through the Book Publishing Industry Development Program (BPIDP) for ou publishing activities. We acknowledge the support of the Canada Council for the Arts for our publishing program. W acknowledge the support of the Government of Ontario through the Ontario Media Development Corporatior Ontario Book Initiative.

The Canada Council | Le Conseil des Arts
for the Arts | du Canada

ONTARIO ARTS COUNCIL
CONSEIL DES ARTS DE L'ONTARIO

Library and Archives Canada Cataloguing in Publication

Paxton, James W.
        Joseph Brant and his world : eighteenth-century mohawk warrior and statesman / James Paxton.

Includes bibliographical references and index.
ISBN 978-1-55277-023-8

        1. Brant, Joseph, 1742–1807. 2. Mohawk Indians—Kings and rulers—Biography.
3. Statesmen—Biography. I. Title.

E99.M8B785 2008   970'.0049755'0092   C2008-903403-1

James Lorimer & Company Ltd., Publishers
317 Adelaide Street West, Suite 1002
Toronto, Ontario M5V 1P9
www.lorimer.ca

Printed in China

NIAGARA FALLS PUBLIC LIBRARY

CONTENTS

A NOTE ON TERMINOLOGY

A study of First Peoples ought to be attentive to language. For obvious reasons, modern historians who employ terms like "savagery" and "civilization" would and should be excoriated by their peers. Similarly, in exploring the life of Joseph Brant, I have come to believe the terms Indian and White are pernicious holdovers from the colonial era. These polarizing racial terms cannot accurately convey the pervasiveness and depth of interaction between cultures. Therefore, Indian and White will not be used, except where the context warrants or in reference to institutions such as the Indian Department. Where possible I will use the names of specific groups — Mohawks, Mississaugas, Scots–Irish — or refer to First Peoples and First Nations.

As First Peoples exert greater influence over the writing of their own history, scholars need to pay attention to the language, concepts, and values that structure their societies. As a result, I will use Six Nations or Haudenosaunee (Ho-de-no-sau-nee) in preference to the more familiar Iroquois, a derisive Algonquian-Basque hybrid word meaning "the killer people." Not surprisingly, that name has fallen out of favour with modern Haudenosaunee. I will, however, use the term Iroquoian when speaking of the broader cultural group to which the Mohawks and other members of the Six Nations belonged, and Iroquoia to refer to the Haudenosaunee homeland. I will continue, however, to employ the term Mohawk instead of Kanien'kehake, meaning the People of the Flint, so as not to overburden the reader with unfamiliar and linguistically challenging words and because many modern Kanien'kehake refer to themselves as Mohawks.

CHAPTER 1
JOSEPH BRANT'S WORLD

In March 1743, as the warm rays of an early spring sun imperceptibly loosened winter's grip on the lands and people of the Ohio River Valley, a woman named Margaret gave birth to a baby boy. Far from her Mohawk Valley home, Margaret and her husband Peter Tehowaghwengaraghkwin had been in the Ohio country for a year or less. Surrounded by people from different nations speaking foreign languages, Margaret named the child Thayendanegea (Tai-yen-da-nay-geh), a word that in the Mohawk language signifies "two sticks of wood bound together." The name was apt. Not only did it connect the boy with his mother's people, but Haudenosaunee orators also frequently referred to bundles of sticks as a metaphor for strength and interdependence. A single stick snaps easily; the same stick when bundled with others acquires resiliency. Throughout his life, Thayendanegea would seek strength and well-being by cultivating mutually beneficial alliances with other people.

Thayendanegea would become one of the most famous Aboriginal men of his day, and although he would continue to use his Mohawk name, modern Canadians and Americans know him by his Christian name, Joseph Brant. It was as Joseph Brant that he won fame for skillfully leading parties of warriors and Loyalist soldiers during the American Revolution. After Britain's defeat in that war, it was as Joseph Brant that he led elements of the Six Nations who refused to live within the new United States to what would become Upper Canada. If Canadians were so inclined, they might think of him as one of the founders of Ontario. And it was as Joseph Brant that he became a

An Iroquoian family in the late eighteenth century.

The Mohawk River, winding through Montgomery County, near Little Falls, New York.

recognized leader and spokesperson for his people. For twenty years after the revolution, until his death in 1807, Brant's tumultuous relationship with other Six Nations' leaders and Great Britain generated recriminations, the echoes of which have become part of his legacy.

Brant remains a controversial and enigmatic character. Some historians read into the two names Thayendanegea and Joseph Brant the tensions and contradictions First Peoples faced and continue to face living under colonialism. How can we understand someone like Brant, who learned how to read and write, worshipped in an Anglican church, and seemed to move effortlessly between Mohawk and English societies? Was he as his major biographer Isabel Kelsay and many modern Haudenosaunee contend, someone who kept a foot in two irreconcilable worlds without being fully part of either?

Brant, I argue, was neither unique nor so internally divided. For more than a century before his birth, the Mohawk people had been adapting and incorporating Dutch, French, and English influences into their own distinct and dynamic culture. Rather than a man straddling two worlds, Brant, like the Mohawk people, embodied a whole but distinct culture that emerged from the contact and interaction of diverse people. The twin names,

Thayendanegea and Joseph Brant, succinctly distil the personality and life experiences of the man and his people. But before assessing Brant and the choices he made, we must first understand the world he inhabited.

Thayendanegea's humble origins and the passage of time have obscured his early life, so that scholars know little about his parents and almost nothing about his childhood. Neither Margaret nor Peter Tehowaghwengaraghkwin performed acts of sufficient public importance to have drawn attention to themselves or their children. Some of Brant's contemporaries maintained that he had an English father. The claim cannot be substantiated, but race-conscious Anglo-Americans believed mixed parentage explained Brant's easy acceptance of "civilized" English ways. John Norton, Brant's associate later in life, claimed Margaret and Tehowaghwengaraghkwin were Wendat (Huron) captives that the Mohawks had adopted. While plausible, the assertion is impossible to verify. Nor does the real answer matter very much. Margaret, whether a Mohawk by birth or adoption, was still a Mohawk, and so were her children. Among the matrilineal Mohawks, mothers not fathers determined their children's clan affiliation and nationality. More importantly, when Margaret named her son Thayendanegea, she self-identified as a Mohawk and hoped her son would too.

Before moving west, Margaret and her husband had lived at Canajoharie, one of two Mohawk towns — the other was Tiononderoge — situated on the Mohawk River of what would become central New York State. Margaret and Tehowaghwengaraghkwin married some time before 1741. Together they had at least three children, but Margaret may have had a daughter by another man, making Tehowaghwengaraghkwin Margaret's second husband. Baptismal records kept by the Anglican minister at Fort Hunter's Queen Anne's Chapel, near Tiononderoge, indicate that one or more Mohawk women named Margaret had children baptized in the 1730s and 1740s. If these Margarets are the same person, and if she was also Thayendanegea's mother, then Thayendanegea had at least three older siblings. The eldest, Degonwadonti (Someone Lends Her a Flower), better known to the English as Mary or Molly, was probably born in 1735 or 1736. She may have had a different father than Thayendanegea, but the Mohawks would have considered them full brother and sister. In July 1741 and again in January 1742, Margaret and Tehowaghwengaraghkwin had children, a son named Jacob and a daughter named Christina, baptized at Queen Anne's Chapel. Like many Aboriginal children, Jacob and Christina probably died in infancy. It was soon after Christina's baptism that Margaret, pregnant with her fourth child, and Tehowaghwengaraghkwin left Canajoharie for the west. Although the reasons for the move cannot be known, members of the Six Nations commonly went to the Ohio either to hunt or settle. The loss of two children may also have prompted the move. Whatever their purpose, soon after arriving, Margaret gave birth to Thayendanegea.

Baby Thayendanegea was a member of his mother's wolf clan. Margaret, not Tehowaghwengaraghkwin, was the central figure in the household, a fact that deeply disturbed many Europeans. Clans, headed by powerful clan mothers and composed of many families, structured Iroquoian society and provided an ideal model of human relations. Until the end of the seventeenth century, the senior woman in Mohawk villages lived together with her sisters and daughters, and their husbands and children, within a long, narrow building

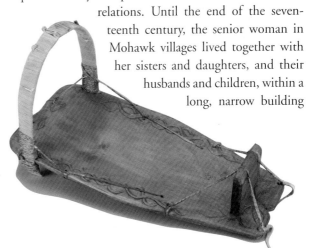

Mohawk mothers worked with their babies on their backs in cradleboards like the one depicted here.

called a longhouse. Reciprocity governed all aspects of life. Women of the same family worked side by side in the fields growing the "Three Sisters," the staple foods of corn, beans, and squash, while their men hunted game, protected the village, or engaged in diplomacy. By Thayendanegea's day, Mohawks had abandoned the longhouses for single-family cabins, but reciprocal obligations still tightly bound family and clan members. Duty compelled everyone to assist kinfolk in need, provide hospitality, and perform certain ritual requirements for other clan members, especially at times of death.

Haudenosaunee concepts of kinship structured other important aspects of society, including the Great League of Peace and Power. Although often confused with a centralized governing institution, the League was, in fact, a body charged with preserving peace and unity among the member nations. Founded by the Peacemaker and his assistant Hiawatha in the decades before European contact, the League embraced the Mohawks, Oneidas, Onondagas, Cayugas, Senecas, and later the Tuscaroras of Carolina, who joined about 1722. Fifty hereditary chiefs, also known as sachems, appointed by the clan mothers, presided over the League, and it was their job to conduct the rituals and oversee the gift exchanges that promoted harmony. In no sense were sachems politicians with coercive powers. Sachems could entreat, cajole, and persuade; they could not command. Members likened the League to a great longhouse — Haudenosaunee means People of the Longhouse — wherein the five, later six, nations resided like members of an extended family.

Speakers exchanged strings of purple and white wampum shells during council meetings to demonstrate that what they said was true.

As the eastern and westernmost nations respectively, the Mohawks and Senecas guarded the doors to the Longhouse. In the centre resided the Onondagas, who kept the council fire burning bright and clear and preserved the purple and white shell wampum belts that recorded the transactions of the League.

By the end of the seventeenth century, sustained contact with various European powers made it necessary for the Haudenosaunee to develop a parallel body to the League that would deal with external issues of diplomacy, trade, and military alliances. The Confederacy, like the League, was not a government that could enforce its decisions; rather, it operated on the principals of unity and consensus. The leadership of the Confederacy, however, was more fluid than that of the League and consisted not just of sachems but also of prominent warriors, elders, and headmen the English often called chiefs.

The League exerted little influence over the lives of Margaret and her family while they lived in the Ohio country. However, a tragedy would force them to return to Mohawk country and to the traditions of their people. Some time after Thayendanegea's birth, his father Tehowaghwengaraghkwin succumbed to disease — probably during one of the many epidemics that scythed through First Nations' communities — leaving Margaret to care for two young children. Mohawks believed that people without kin were virtual non-persons, wholly lacking a social identity. Rather than struggle to survive among strangers, Margaret sought the safety and security of family on the Mohawk River. By 1746, she had returned with Molly and Thayendanegea to Canajoharie.

Canajoharie, together with Tiononderoge thirty miles downstream, replaced towns destroyed during the 1693 French invasion of Mohawk country in what is today central New York State. These newer Mohawk villages lacked the visual impact of their predecessors, which had been constructed to house as many as a thousand people within several enormous longhouses protected by a bristling fence

Top: The interior of a recreated longhouse. Two families shared each firepit and slept in the bunks lining the walls. Bottom: The bark-covered exterior of the longhouse.

of wooden posts. These palisades prompted Europeans to describe the villages as castles. The shift from compact, defensible villages composed of multi-family longhouses to decentralized towns of single-family cabins took place because the Mohawk population collapsed in the seventeenth century. Chronic warfare, epidemics, and out-migration of Catholic converts to Canada reduced the Mohawk population living in the Mohawk Valley from an estimated high of about seven thousand people in the 1630s to about six hundred in 1700, and it hovered there for most of the century. Shattered families abandoned their former village sites, now associated with disease and death, and settled at Canajoharie and Tiononderoge. As the two principal towns of the Mohawk people, Canajoharie and Tiononderoge together housed most of the Mohawks living in the Mohawk Valley.

By the middle decades of the eighteenth century, Canajoharie consisted of a loose collection of forty or fifty cabins scattered along the south side of the Mohawk River about sixty-five miles west of Albany. The word Canajoharie signifies a "pot that washes itself," a reference to a distinctive circular hole scoured into the slate by the rushing waters of nearby Canajoharie Creek. The village Thayendanegea and his family inhabited looked little different from most

The three Mohawks and a Mahican on this and the next page met with Queen Anne in 1710. Mistakenly described as "kings,"
they set the precedent followed by Brant and other Mohawks of travelling to London on diplomatic missions.
Left: Tee Yee Neen Ho Ga Row, baptized Hendrick; right: Sa Ga Yeath Qua Pieth, baptized Brant.

frontier communities. Only the continuing practice of locating the fireplace in the middle of the cabin distinguished Mohawk homes from settler cabins.

Canajoharie's unprepossessing appearance belied its significance. Two related facts, one geographical and the other political, drew people to the village from across America and Europe. Rising in the Adirondack Mountains and meandering gently towards the southwest for 140 miles until its waters mingled with the Hudson River, the Mohawk River forms one of the few major east-west

passes through the Appalachian Mountains. Moreover, proximity to other major river systems — those of the Hudson, the Susquehanna, the Delaware, and and the St. Lawrence rivers — connected the Mohawk to a watery network of highways that carried goods and people across half the continent. As the eastern door of the Longhouse, the Mohawks regulated movement on one of early America's most important thoroughfares and controlled access to the Haudenosaunee homeland, Iroquoia, and the lands beyond. Iroquoia itself was strategically important.

Left: Etow Oh Koam, a Mahican, baptized Nicholas; right: Ho Nee Yeath Taw No Row, baptized John.

Flanked by New France to the north and English New York to the east, the Six Nations leveraged their position in between rival empires to great political and economic advantage. Courted by two ardent and generous suitors, the French and the English, the Six Nations flirted with both but committed to neither. This policy of neutrality served the Six Nations well for the first half of the eighteenth century, enhancing Mohawk power and influence despite their small numbers. The potent combination of geography and politics brought to the Mohawks' doorsteps any number of traders, soldiers, missionaries, diplomats, and curiosity seekers.

Until 1710, most visitors to Mohawk country either passed through or stayed a short while before returning home. The next year, however, men arrived and began work on a fort and mission at Fort Hunter near Tiononderoge. Soon after, British soldiers and a missionary moved in. The Mohawks had requested the minister as a sign of English friendship and the fort for protection during the War of Spanish Succession (1702–1713), one of several eighteenth-century European conflicts that had North American theatres. The presence of the garrison, however, had rekindled fears that the Mohawks were losing control of their land. Victims of New York's

Mohawk River passing through a region called the Noses near Canajoharie, New York.

black-coated ministers had arrived, the Mohawk Valley witnessed an even greater influx of Europeans set on making the region their home. These newcomers would profoundly alter the region's demographics and shape the world that Thayendanegea would inherit. In the winter of 1712–1713, six German-speaking men approached the Mohawks for permission to settle in the Schoharie Valley, a tributary of the Mohawk, with their families and friends. It was a bold request. Surprisingly, the Mohawks consented.

One reason the Mohawks may have agreed to the appeal for land was the pitiful story the Germans told. The six men explained that, three years earlier, deteriorating economic conditions had forced them, along with thousands of their countrymen, to leave their homes in southwestern Germany. They went first to England, where they received food and shelter until politicians blanched at the mounting costs to the treasury and herded them aboard ships bound for New York. When they arrived in New York City in the summer of 1710, Governor Robert Hunter rounded up the Palatines, as the Germans had come to be known, and sent them to work camps on the Hudson River, where they were to labour making tar and pitch for the Royal Navy until they had repaid the Crown for their upkeep and passage to America. The Palatines, who had come to believe that they were to be given land in a place called the Schoharie Valley, were bitterly disappointed. The mistake arose because Hunter, who had invested heavily in the project, had scouted the Schoharie Valley as a possible location for the work camps, but had dismissed the site as unsuitable. For the next two

notoriously corrupt land-granting system, Mohawks had watched as royal governors had rewarded favourites with extravagant grants of their land. Outraged Mohawks had denied the legitimacy of these claims, and a subsequent governor, the Earl of Bellomont, repealed several of the most egregious grants. Mohawks were naturally wary about the prospects of losing their land.

Only a year after the red-jacketed British soldiers and

years, the Palatines lived and worked in conditions so wretched they compared their lot to the Israelites held in bondage in Egypt and looked to Schoharie as the Promised Land. The tar-making scheme went bankrupt in 1712, and the Palatines acted on the opportunity to obtain the long unseen Schoharie lands. Hunter was furious at losing his investment and his workforce.

Listening to the Palatines' story, the Mohawks sensed an opportunity to pre-empt the fraudulent land claims of arrogant Englishmen by planting poor and deserving Germans on the disputed lands. That the Palatines were isolated, friendless, and distrusted by New York officials meant they would depend on the Mohawks to defend their interests and landholdings. Better to have neighbours of one's choosing, the Mohawks reasoned, and if those neighbours were also dependants, all the better.

By the spring of 1713, perhaps a hundred and fifty German-speaking families lived scattered throughout the Schoharie Valley. Despite the real cultural differences separating the two peoples, the common fear of dispossession drew Mohawks and Germans together. Mohawks helped the newcomers adjust to the unfamiliar landscape, showing them where and how to gather edible nuts, berries, and roots and to grow the Three Sisters. Without this aid, many Palatines would have perished in the hungry months of late winter and early spring. As the Palatines blended Mohawk strategies for living on the land with European crops and agricultural techniques, they became well-adapted to their new environment.

In learning to live on the land, the Palatines also learned how to live with the Mohawks. One settler, John Conrad Weiser, recognizing that his family's survival would depend on cultivating good relations with people who seemed

utterly foreign, sent his son to live with the Mohawks for language training. Once locals had breached a the language barrier, relationships based on mutual self-interest blossomed into friendships. Mohawks and Germans visited each other's homes, conducted small-scale trade, and socialized in taverns and trading posts. The popularity of taverns, in fact, became a source of complaint. Chiefs objected that young men were becoming much addicted to alcohol, and unfortunate individuals who lived within earshot of these taverns complained of the noise. No one it seems took these complaints seriously, however, as Mohawks and Germans continued to drink together, much to the annoyance of the neighbours. Some Palatines even learned to perform the most important of Haudenosaunee rituals, the Condolence Ceremony. The Condolence soothed and calmed families that had lost a member to death. Iroquoian people believed that not attending to powerful emotions led to anti-social and even violent behaviour.

Many Mohawks saw much that they admired and found worthy of borrowing among their German neighbours. Canajoharies began renting land to Palatine families too poor to purchase their own. Two advantages that leases had over sales were that they kept the land in Canajoharie hands and they generated revenue. Some Mohawk households began using iron hoes and ploughs to plant wheat and oats beside the Three Sisters. Cows and sheep grazed in Mohawk fields, while pigs snuffled and rooted in nearby pens. With the profits earned from the sale of surplus grain and meat to Albany, some wealthy individuals built frame houses that would have made middle-class Englishmen proud. Few Mohawks lived this grandly, but during the American Revolution, American Colonel Peter Gansevoort would report, "The Indians live much better than most of the

Mohawk River farmers." The introduction of market-oriented agriculture did not overturn the redistributive economy. Generosity and hospitality remained cherished and necessary values.

···❖···

The arrangements worked out by Mohawks and Palatines in the early decades of the eighteenth century provided the model by which subsequent immigrants were acculturated into the local culture. A second wave of Germans came to the valley in the 1720s, and the Scots–Irish followed in the 1730s and 1740s. By and large, these groups conformed to local practices and adjusted well to the region's multicultural makeup. Thayendanegea knew no other world. He was too young to remember a time when the Mohawk Valley belonged exclusively to the Mohawk people. For him and others of his generation, diversity, the presence of German and Scots–Irish neighbours, was the natural order of things.

Not content to let the river wash people onto their shores, Canajoharies engaged actively with the world beyond the Mohawk Valley. Diplomats journeyed to New York, Philadelphia, Quebec, and occasionally to London; hunters carried skins and furs to Albany; warriors ranged deep into Carolina to raid their old enemies the Catawbas. The success or failure of Mohawk men in these activities — and these were exclusively male activities — brought prestige or shame to their home villages, but they also directly affected the lives of women and children.

Soon after returning to Canajoharie, Margaret had married for the second, or perhaps the third, time. The match was a good one. Margaret's new husband was a prominent war leader named Lykas, who could both support her young family and raise their status in Canajoharie society. The marriage seemed fruitful at first. Margaret bore two children, Jacomine in 1747 and Lea in 1750, but both children died in infancy. Tragedy struck again the

year of Lea's birth; Lykas perished while leading a raid against the Catawbas of Carolina.

Margaret would not starve or want for necessities as long as she had kin nearby. Besides, women were the farmers of the Mohawk people, and, she could by her own labour provide for her children. But Lykas had hunted and traded furs for the manufactured goods on which the Mohawks had become dependent. In order to obtain kettles, knives, beads, and cloth, she would have to earn money.

For cash, Margaret turned to the ginseng trade. During the 1750s, overseas demand for the medicinal plant sent prices soaring to over thirty shillings a pound on the London market, sparking a ginseng craze in New York, where the plant grew wild. Doubtless, Thayendanegea and Molly assisted their mother while she scoured the forests beyond the river for the crimson berries that marked the presence of the valuable roots hidden below the soil's surface. While digging for ginseng, Margaret encountered two men who would have a profound influence on her and her family.

The first was William Johnson, who had helped to fuel the obsession with ginseng in the Mohawk Valley by buying as much of the root as the Mohawks could gather. A native of County Meath, Ireland, Johnson had come to America at the behest of his uncle, Peter Warren. Warren had acquired thirteen thousand acres in the Mohawk Valley and wanted to turn the tract into a profitable tenant community. The settlement, variously named Warrenbush or Warrenburgh, lay south of the Mohawk River a few miles from Tiononderoge. Johnson aspired to be more than a manager, and he soon entered into the traditional frontier pursuits of land speculation and the fur trade. By 1739, he had purchased land and opened a trading post across the river from Warrenbush and began competing directly with the large Albany merchants. Mohawks preferred to deal with the ambitious but honest Irishman rather than the Albany merchants. Soon they began addressing Johnson with the fitting name Warraghiyagey, or "He Who Does Much Business." In 1749, with the

Schenectady boats, so called because they were built in Schenectady, New York, during the eighteenth century, carried the Mohawk Valley's surplus grain and meat to market.
Opposite, top: Ginseng root.

profits he earned from furs, Johnson built a mansion, a three-storey stone edifice appropriately named Fort Johnson, on the north bank of the Mohawk River. For Johnson, the ginseng trade was a natural extension of his other economic activities. And it was while purchasing bags of the roots that he probably first caught a glimpse of Margaret's teenaged daughter Molly. In less than a decade, the two would be living as husband and wife.

Searching for ginseng, Margaret also met a fellow forager, much older than herself, named Brant Kanagaradunckwa. Until this time, the two had probably never met — he lived at Tiononderoge and she at Canajoharie — but Margaret almost certainly knew that this man was a turtle clan sachem and one of the wealthiest men at Tiononderoge. Unlike many sachems who impoverished themselves by giving away possessions to maintain and attract followers, Kanagaradunckwa had built himself a two-storey frame house appointed with all the luxuries of any middle-class English home. Guests declared his lodgings and hospitality first rate: "There was nothing wanting in our food or drink or in our beds." Kanagaradunckwa, too, had recently lost his spouse, and this shared experience may have brought them closer. The widow and widower began a relationship, and soon Margaret announced that she was pregnant.

In March 1753, Margaret presented an infant son to Rev. John Ogilvie, the Anglican minister serving at Queen Anne's Chapel, for baptism. She named the child Jacob. Ogilvie, of course, frowned on illegitimacy, which the Mohawks did not consider sinful, and demanded to know the father's name. When Margaret admitted that Kanagaradunckwa had fathered the child, the answer shocked the community. In addition to the age and differences in status between the two, Kanagaradunckwa had scandalized his dead wife's family by refusing to follow custom and marry his sister-in-law. Perhaps to escape the wrath of his inlaws, Kanagaradunckwa abandoned his fine home and moved to Canajoharie. In September, a relieved Ogilvie presided over Margaret and Kanagaradunckwa's marriage; ten-year-old Thayendanegea acquired his third father.

After Kanagaradunckwa moved into Margaret's household, locals began calling Thayendanegea "Joseph Thayendanegea" or "Brant's Joseph," linking the lad with his sachem stepfather. He had probably received Joseph as his christening name after the return to Canajoharie; Margaret had him baptized by one of the local ministers, perhaps, like many Mohawks, believing that the holy water would protect her child through life. Among Mohawks, Brant was a common first name that probably derived from Dutch or German names such as Barent or Brandt. In time, Brant's Joseph morphed into Joseph Brant. This later permutation may have come from the lips of neighbouring German- and English-speaking settlers, who had their own conventions when it came to naming children.

Marrying Kanagaradunckwa had established Margaret and her children in the upper ranks of Mohawk society, but it did not make her life easier. Kanagaradunckwa's presence brought a steady stream of visitors into Margaret's house. As a sachem, he opened his doors to many people and ensured his guests never left hungry. But it was Margaret, Molly, and their female relatives who grew and prepared the food that underwrote his hospitality. It was hard work, but it conferred respectability and influence.

One of the frequent guests who partook of Margaret's hospitality was William Johnson (Warraghiyagey). Johnson travelled often to Canajoharie on business. Despite living nearer to Tiononderoge, Johnson had developed closer relationships to the leading men and women of Canajoharie. During the day, Johnson bargained and bartered with hunters for their furs and negotiated with chiefs over matters of politics. In both cases, an exchange of gifts beforehand eased the transactions. At night, he retired to Kanagaradunckwa's house, where he renewed his acquaintances with Molly and Thayendanegea. At these times, Thayendanegea observed how reciprocity, hospitality, and gift-giving could broker alliances across cultures.

Thayendanegea's daily life provided similar lessons. Compared with English parents, Mohawk mothers and fathers gave their children considerable independence and freedom to investigate the world around them. As he grew older, Brant and his friends began to range beyond the village for days, or perhaps weeks, at a time, exploring the sun-drenched fields and meadows near the river bottoms and climbing across the dark, cool forests spreading across the mountain slopes. They spent much of their time shooting deer and bear and catching the trout, pike, and salmon that teemed in the Mohawk and its tributaries, tasks they would take up with more seriousness as they grew into

William Johnson built his second home, Fort Johnson, in 1749, near Amsterdam, New York.
Opposite: Mohawk women adorned their dresses with silver brooches such as this.

men. Indeed, traversing the countryside with guns and fish-hooks, the boys received excellent training as hunters and warriors. During these perambulations, the affable Brant befriended many of the settlers at whose homes he stopped for rest, conversation, and refreshment. In later years, after he had earned the epithet "the Monster" for his activities during the American Revolution, several settlers remembered young Brant fondly. One woman waxed nostalgic as she recalled the Mohawk boy staying with her family for several days so he could play with her brothers, who were about the same age. The youth's "manly bearing" and "noble goodhearted" nature left a deep impression.

The beliefs and values Joseph Brant carried with him through life coalesced from the experiences and lessons instilled in him at Canajoharie. Brant was a Mohawk. But what it meant to be Mohawk in the middle decades of the eighteenth century could not be divorced from the diversity of people and ideas that blended in the Mohawk Valley. Brant lived with multiculturalism long before the term had meaning. If his experiences among German and Scots–Irish settlers did not make him any less Mohawk, he did develop a particular understanding of the world, one his immediate neighbours shared. From experience, Brant knew differences between people could be a source of strength.

CHAPTER 2
STORM CLOUDS

War powerfully shaped Joseph Brant's life. Born on the eve of the War of Austrian Succession (1744–1748), he came of age during the Seven Years War (1754–1760 in North America) and Pontiac's War (1763–1765), and emerged as a leader in his own right during the American Revolution (1775–1783). After the Revolution, war and rumours of war provided the background and context for the remainder of his life. The half-century of almost constant conflict also profoundly influenced Haudenosaunee society, as warriors like Brant assumed greater power and responsibilities in the affairs of their people.

In 1744, the nations of Europe went to war yet again, this time over who would ascend to the Austrian throne. Fortunately, when the War of Austrian Succession spread to Europe's North American colonies, Margaret, Tehowaghwengaraghkwin, Molly, and Thayendanegea were living in the Ohio country, a safe distance from the fighting. Their kinfolk and friends in the Mohawk Valley,

however, occupied the dangerous middle ground between the belligerent empires. For the first two years of the war, the Six Nations' policy of neutrality held, despite pleas from New York for military assistance. The failure of the Albany Indian Commissioners, who were also deeply involved in the fur trade, to bring the Six Nations into an active alliance, prompted Governor George Clinton to turn responsibility for Indian affairs over to William Johnson in 1746. Johnson had three qualities Clinton admired. The young Irishman had already defied these same Albany traders, whom Clinton detested for placing their own profits ahead of the Crown's interest by establishing direct trade with the Mohawks; in so doing, he won the Mohawks' confidence. He also supported the governor's pro-war policies because, as a frontier resident exposed to French attack, Johnson's safety and livelihood depended on a vigorous prosecution of the war.

In 1746, Warraghiyagey, dressed and painted in Mohawk fashion, marched into Canajoharie bearing the governor's commission. The trader had become a warrior. His first job was to restore the Covenant Chain, a term both the British and Six Nations used to describe the British-Haudenosaunee alliance. Although many Canajoharies remained sceptical of the war, Johnson's ties to the Mohawks earned him a respectful hearing. Not only had he dealt with them fairly over the years, but he had also claimed a stake in Mohawk society by fathering children with at least two Canajoharie women. At the same time, he lived with a German woman named Catherine Weisenberg, who had borne him three more children.

Six Nations' knife and decorated sheath.

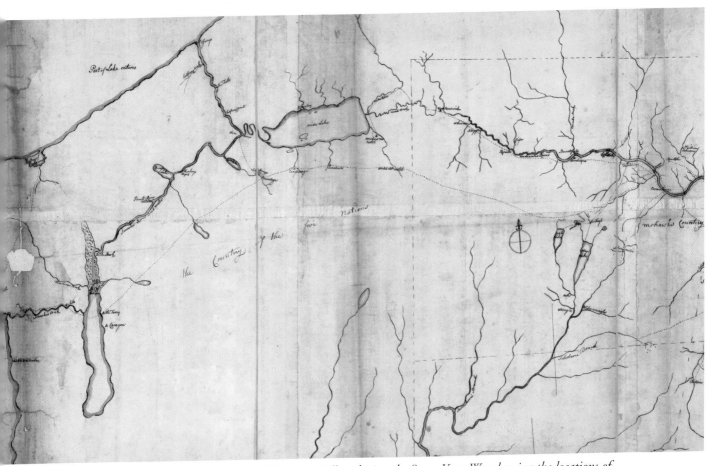

A detailed map of the Oswego, Onondaga, and Mohawk Valleys during the Seven Years War showing the locations of Aboriginal and Euro-American settlements.

Surrounded by eager listeners, Warraghiyagey exhorted his kinsmen to meet with Governor George Clinton at Albany, where they would be given the war hatchet to use against the French and their Algonquian allies. Johnson finished by distributing gifts and enjoining the young men to perform the war dance with him. Enthralled warriors immediately volunteered to join an expedition against New France.

The war altered Canajoharie in subtle but fundamental ways. Nearby, the wooden palisades of a new fort rose up from freshly turned earth, forming a lasting reminder of the conflict. As war parties returned to their villages, mourners wailed in grief for kinfolk who had fallen victim to French bayonets and Algonquian scalping knives. Warriors who survived, however, paraded through town in rich tunics, silver gorgets, and braided hats, carrying new well-oiled guns as the visible symbols of their friendship with the English king. By contrast, poor sachems, whose mandate was to achieve peace, reaped relatively few rewards from wartime alliances.

Margaret would have noticed that Canajoharie's political landscape had also changed. In particular, Theyanoguin, known to the English as Hendrick Peters or more usually as Hendrick, who had long figured prominently in both local and Confederacy politics, now commanded much more influence and authority. A League sachem, Hendrick had linked his fortunes with those of William Johnson and had prospered. Johnson lavished him with presents purchased at public expense. He in turn redistributed the bounty to warriors. As a result, Hendrick became the primary mediator between the Mohawks and English.

Above: Theyanoguin (Hendrick) in 1740, wearing the signs of his alliance with Britain, a laced hat and coat. Note the facial tattoos.
Right: William Johnson commonly gave silver gorgets as presents to warriors.

·⁙·

The War of Austrian Succession ended in 1748. With the colony's borders secure, New York's Assembly returned to its stingy ways and cut spending on Indian affairs. As the Mohawks' usefulness as allies waned, so too did the flow of British goods. Feeling slighted by his erstwhile allies, Hendrick flirted with generous French agents. Johnson also grew dissatisfied with what he saw as the colony's chronic underfunding of Indian affairs. Disgusted at having to dip into his own private fortune to keep the Six Nations in the English interest, Johnson resigned. When Clinton promised to replace Johnson, Hendrick fumed that no such replacement could be found as "one half of Coll: Johnson belonged to his Excellency and the other half to [the Mohawks]." As the chief predicted, no suitable replacement could be located, and the Albany Indian Commissioners resumed their work.

The restoration of peace renewed the interest of many colonists in acquiring western land. By the middle decades of the eighteenth century, the Mohawks' small population and large land base made them easy targets for land fraud. Several incidents proved especially vexing. Kayaderosseras, a tract of land between the Hudson and Mohawk rivers amounting to several hundreds of thousand of acres, became the subject of a long-standing dispute between the Mohawks and a consortium of land speculators who claimed the tract through a fraudulent patent. Closer to home, Canajoharies contended with New York City merchant Philip Livingston and his Albany partners who, it was said, had got several chiefs drunk to obtain their signatures on a deed that included the Mohawks' riverfront planting lands. At the same time, Tiononderoge confronted the Corporation of Albany, which held a deed to the lands beneath the village. A number of disagreements concerning smaller amounts of land embroiled the Mohawks in rancorous disputes with their German neighbours. Characteristically, colonial authorities ignored Mohawk complaints.

Mohawk grievances against the colony accumulated

A painting of the French fort of Carillon on Lake Champlain, which was taken by the English and renamed Fort Ticonderoga.

until, in 1753, Hendrick led a delegation to New York City. The old sachem upbraided Clinton for ignoring his allies. When Clinton brushed aside the complaints, Hendrick announced, "The Covenant Chain is broken between you and us. So brother you are not to expect to hear of me any more, and Brother we desire to hear no more of you." With that, the Mohawk delegates turned on their heels and went home, leaving Clinton the unenviable task of relating what had just transpired to his superiors in London.

Hendrick's announcement fell like a thunderclap, reverberating across the Atlantic and through the corridors of Whitehall. The Mohawks had been Britain's only reliable allies in the northeast, and the breaking of the Covenant Chain came at a time when the French were aggressively fortifying their holdings in the Ohio region against the land claims of the Virginia-based Ohio Company. Virginia planters and land speculators, including Governor Robert Dinwiddie and a young George Washington, were prepared to fight the French for land they believed was theirs. Forgotten in this intercolonial

rivalry were the region's inhabitants, the Shawnee and Delaware, who also prepared to defend their homes. Realizing that the three-way contest for land in the distant Ohio threatened to draw the Empire into war, the Board of Trade, whose job it was to supervise colonial affairs, ordered troops to America and centralized Indian affairs.

When General Edward Braddock, the new commander-in-chief for America, disembarked in 1755, he carried with him two commissions made out to William Johnson. The first promoted Johnson to major general in command of an expedition to capture the French fort of Carillon at Crown Point guarding the southern tip of Lake Champlain. The second gave Johnson sole responsibility for negotiating with the Six Nations. The following year, the Crown expanded his powers further by naming him Superintendent of Indian Affairs in the northern colonies. The Board of Trade noted specifically that Johnson's long tenure among the Mohawks and his knowledge of their "manners and customs" uniquely qualified him for this

The Fall of Braddock. *A portrayal of the defeat of British General Edward Braddock near Fort Duquesne, July 1755. Opposite, top: Christian Daniel Claus, painted in the 1770s, became deputy superintendent for Canada after the Seven Years' War and married Ann Johnson, Sir William's daughter. He was a close friend and ally of Joseph Brant. Opposite, below: Haudenosaunee hunters would have received weapons like this English trade gun from British merchants.*

most important post. The outbreak of the Seven Years War placed Johnson firmly in charge and returned the Mohawks to the centre of British Indian policy.

One of Johnson's first acts as superintendent was to meet with the Six Nations and their neighbours at his home, Fort Johnson. The conference opened on June 21 with over one thousand people in attendance. Doubtless, twelve-year-old Joseph Brant was there and, together with the other Canajoharie boys, darted in and out of the throngs of colourfully dressed people who crowded into the mansion and its outbuildings and spilled out over the lawns. Once deliberations began, he would have quietly watched as solemn orators rose and delivered carefully prepared speeches, all the while fingering strings and wampum belts to jog their memories. Johnson, too, art-

fully responded, invoking Haudenosaunee images of growing trees and bundled sticks that signified unity and alliance to exhort the Six Nations to join Great Britain in the war against the French. After the day's proceedings, young Brant might have caught snatches of private conversations between Johnson and headmen. It was in the bushes away from the formal deliberations that the real negotiations took place. On the last day of the council, the Six Nations gave assurances that they would strike the French. They then divided £1,100 worth of presents and went home. A diplomatic triumph, the conference had apparently achieved more than Johnson had dared hope.

Within a month, however, British military bungling had cancelled out almost all of Johnson's gains. In July, Braddock lost his life and two-thirds of his army to a smaller French force near Fort Duquesne (now Pittsburgh). The stunning defeat had a sobering effect on the Haudenosaunee who, having just returned home laden down with Johnson's presents, began to have second thoughts about the wisdom of their decision. Not surprisingly, only Mohawks volunteered in substantial numbers for the 1755 campaign against Fort St. Frédéric at Crown Point.

On reaching Lake George, south of Lake Champlain, Johnson pushed a detachment of provincial troops and warriors straight into a French trap. As the aged and infirm Hendrick led his Mohawk warriors forward, from the dense foliage, pro-French Caughnawaga Mohawks called out, warning the chief of his predicament. Hendrick, however, either did not hear or refused to listen and marched on. Smoke and flame erupted on both sides of the Mohawk party. When the firing stopped, Hendrick and forty warriors lay dead. The French commander, ebullient at his initial success, pursued the frightened provincials and surviving Mohawks back towards Johnson's main army. British artillery barred the way, flaying French ranks with grapeshot and stopping the advance. Later, soldiers found the French commander mortally wounded in front of the guns. Victory-starved Britons rewarded Johnson with £5,000 and a baronetcy, even though a painful wound in the thigh incapacitated him for most of the battle. The loss of Hendrick, however, tempered Johnson's triumph.

News of the ambush cast the Mohawks into deep mourning. The loss of so many warriors devastated Canajoharie and Tiononderoge. Few families remained untouched by death. Margaret, who had lost Lykas in an earlier war, would have joined the bereaved. All activities stopped until the funerary rights had been completed and the Condolence Ceremony performed over the grieving families, and a new chief installed to replace Hendrick.

Hendrick's death was a massive blow to Johnson. Without his friend and ally, he could not count on Mohawk support for subsequent campaigns. Following the Crown Point fiasco, Tiononderoge virtually withdrew its support from the war, as the women and sachems resisted all efforts to mobilize the warriors. When the governor asked warriors to participate in the next upcoming campaign, one chief replied sarcastically that he should ask the five upper nations, whose pro- French proclivities were well known. The people of Canajoharie felt their losses just as keenly, but familial ties to Johnson blunted criticism. For the next four years, Johnson tried with limited success to conduct Indian affairs without close and powerful allies among the Mohawks.

Kanagaradunckwa continued to support his friend. Although he was too old to fight, his fifteen-year-old stepson, Joseph Brant, and some other Mohawks volunteered to join their British allies. In the summer of 1758, Brant set out on his first military campaign, joining General James Abercromby's expedition against Fort Carillon, which the British later renamed Fort Ticonderoga. If Brant hoped to see action, he was disappointed. Except for some minor skirmishing, the warriors did not enter combat.

When the battle opened on July 8, they watched in relative safety from a nearby hill as British regulars dashed themselves to pieces against an entrenched French enemy. Glad to have avoided another British debacle, the Mohawks took their presents and went home.

Three of Johnson's lieutenants also witnessed Abercromby's discouraging defeat. Daniel Claus, Guy Johnson, and John Butler had joined the campaign and, doubtless, became acquainted with Brant. Not one of them, however, could have guessed how intertwined their lives would become with that of the teenaged Mohawk. Of the three, Brant knew Claus the best. The German-born Claus had arrived at Canajoharie in 1750 with the intention of learning the Mohawk language. The budding linguist soon came to the attention of William Johnson, who commissioned him as a lieutenant in the Indian Department and employed him as a secretary. Later Claus married Johnson's daughter Ann, who was better known as Nancy. Although Claus was sixteen years Brant's senior, the two men became close friends. Claus's companion, Guy Johnson, was a little older than Brant. Born in Ireland and claiming

Walter Butler, the father of John Butler, built the Butler House in 1743 near Fonda, New York.

kinship with William Johnson, Guy also served in the Indian Department as a secretary and later as a deputy agent. He married another of Johnson's daughters, Mary, who went by the nickname Polly.

With Claus and Johnson was John Butler. Butler's father, a lieutenant in the British army, had moved his family to the Mohawk Valley when he was posted to Fort Hunter. John Butler immersed himself in the local culture, learning Mohawk and perhaps other Native languages as well. Butler worked for Johnson as an interpreter and eventually received a captaincy in the Indian Department. Of all Johnson's subordinates, Butler was the most capable.

By 1759, William Johnson had built significant new bridges to the Mohawks. In that year, he and Molly Brant

began living together as husband and wife. Local tradition holds that Johnson fell in love with Molly Brant while attending a militia muster. The young woman leapt into the saddle behind a militia officer and rode around the parade ground with her dark tresses streaming in the wind. The real story is probably far more prosaic. Johnson had known Molly Brant from his many visits to Kanagaradunckwa's house. It was probably during one of these visits that she became pregnant. She gave birth to a son, Peter Warren Johnson, named for Johnson's uncle.

Arriving at Fort Johnson with her newborn baby some time in 1759, Brant moved into the household either just before or immediately after the death of Catherine Weisenberg, Johnson's long-time partner and the mother of his three children, Ann, Mary, and John. What the

Peter Warren Johnson, the eldest son of Molly Brant and William Johnson, as an adult.

Guy Johnson, ca. 1760, about the time he was promoted deputy agent of Indian affairs and married Mary Johnson, Sir William's daughter.

Johnson children, then in their late teens and early twenties, thought of the young Mohawk woman who took charge of the household so soon after their mother had been committed to the ground is unknown. Betraying no misgivings about entering the rarefied world of the baronet, Brant, a powerful woman in her own right, soon stamped an indelible mark on Fort Johnson. By contrast, Weisenberg had exerted little discernible influence and barely warranted mention in Johnson's correspondence. Brant, however, purchased numerous household goods, ranging from expensive fine china to ordinary kitchenware and sewing supplies. She oversaw the manor's large staff and saw to the needs of a steady stream of visitors. The latter chore had both social and political dimensions, as many visitors arrived on diplomatic business.

Brant managed domestic affairs with skill and grace, but neither she nor Johnson expected the domestic duties to occupy all of her time. As a clan mother, Brant doubtless played an active, if not always visible, role in political discussions. In part, this was possible because Haudenosaunee men did not share Europeans' disdain for women who spoke their minds. Indeed, as a clan mother and the wife of Britain's Indian Superintendent, men would have sought her advice and listened attentively to her counsel.

In 1759, British fortunes also began to turn around. Louisbourg fell to British and American troops. British forces captured Fort Frontenac at what is now Kingston,

This drawing of Fort Johnson by Guy Johnson appeared in the October 1759 issue of the Royal Magazine.

Ontario, in August, cutting the supply lines to the Ohio country. Starved French soldiers abandoned Fort Duquesne in November. Sensing a British victory, the Six Nations abandoned their long-held policy of neutrality. In the spring of 1759, seven hundred warriors, representing all six nations of the Confederacy, joined the war's final campaigns against Fort Niagara, Montreal, and Quebec. This was an unprecedented effort, as the Confederacy could muster no more than a thousand warriors.

In June, Joseph Brant and forty other warriors left Canajoharie for Oswego, a British post on the south shore of Lake Ontario, where they rendezvoused with Johnson and nearly a thousand warriors. Three thousand British regulars and American provincials under the command of Brigadier General John Prideaux arrived on the twenty-seventh, and Prideaux set the force in motion for Fort Niagara. Overlooking the juncture of the Niagara River and Lake Ontario, Fort Niagara was the last major French fortress before Montreal. The French commander, Captain Pierre Pouchot, knew nothing of the British march through Iroquoia until Confederacy warriors attacked a work detail outside the fort's walls. On July 10, Prideaux began digging trenches, and the siege began in earnest. Facing only five hundred troops, British trenches pushed steadily forward under the cover of a destructive artillery barrage. When a shell from one of these guns exploded prematurely, killing Prideaux, command devolved upon Johnson.

Six Nations warriors did not perform the dirty work of digging. Rather, Brant and his comrades ranged into the surrounding woods to keep a vigilant watch on the army's flanks and rear. Two weeks into the siege, they spotted a French relief force on the Niagara River above the falls. Together with British regulars and American troops, warriors set up an ambush on the road to Fort Niagara at La Belle Famille (Youngstown). In the woods beside the road, Brant may well have received his first experience of combat.

Above: The church Notre-Dame-de-la-Victoire, Quebec City, lay in ruins after conquest in 1759, as depicted here by artist Richard Short. Below: An English medal awarded to Native allies who accompanied Amherst's army to Montreal.

It was a one-sided affair, as the French soldiers charged hopelessly at the well-defended position. The destruction of the French relief force shattered the hopes of Fort Niagara's weary defenders. On July 25, Pouchot accepted Johnson's terms of surrender. Doubtless, Brant was among those who plundered the fort and its storehouses before returning home.

The next summer, Brant was one of seven hundred warriors sent by the various nations of the Confederacy to capture Montreal. The young Mohawk again trekked to Oswego, where British General Jeffrey Amherst was assembling an army of eleven thousand men. Crammed into boats, bateaux, and canoes, the army began its advance on Montreal on August 10.

All went well until the army captured Fort Lévis on the St. Lawrence River. Amherst, fearing a massacre, forbade the Six Nations from entering the fort, while British soldiers enriched themselves with French plunder. A majority of the Six Nations left in disgust. Brant, however, was one of fewer than two hundred warriors who remained with the army and was part of the capture of Montreal in September. For their efforts, he and the other warriors who persevered received silver medals commemorating their participation in the campaign. The fall of Montreal marked the end of the Seven Years War in America, although the conflict would continue in Europe for another three years.

A view of the Citadel at Quebec in 1784, painted by James Peachey.

Soon after returning home, William Johnson received a letter from Lebanon, Connecticut. The sender, Eleazar Wheelock, was a minister and educator who operated Moor's Charity School, named after the philanthropist who had donated the school's land and buildings. Its mission was to educate the boys of New England's First Nations, in addition to a few Anglo-American youths. In his letter, Wheelock explained that the Society in Scotland for Propagating Christian Knowledge had recently provided funding to educate three Six Nations' youths, and he hoped the superintendent would assent to the scheme. Wheelock's express purpose was to train Aboriginal children to become interpreters or fit them for other occupations of "publick usefulness among their Own Nations." Johnson, of course, saw the value of training Mohawk interpreters and immediately thought of his brother-in-law. Brant already knew a little English, and,

with some education, he could work in the Indian Department.

In July, Brant departed for Connecticut with two other Canajoharie youths, Sander and Nickus. Johnson must have made loyalty, as evidenced in military service, a criterion in selecting suitable candidates, because all three had participated in the Montreal campaign. Arriving on August 1, the new pupils did not make a good first impression. Wheelock noted two of the three students, Sander and Nickus, had arrived nearly naked and lousy and unable to speak any English. Sander was clearly ill. Of the three, only Brant met with the stern minister's approval. He had come well dressed and able to speak a few words of English. These outward signs of "civility," however slim, suggested to Wheelock that Joseph came from a "Family of Distinction."

The three Canajoharies added substantially to the student body, which consisted of a few Delawares, a Mohegan, a Montauk, and Samuel Kirkland, the son of an impoverished Connecticut minister. Kirkland dreamed of becoming a missionary, but could not afford an education. Wheelock had taken him as a charity case. Brant and Kirkland gravitated to one another, as Kirkland wanted to learn Mohawk.

Students followed a rigid daily routine that deliberately contrasted with the relaxed and relatively unstructured lifestyle they had been accustomed to in their home villages. After rising early, pupils attended worship, ate breakfast, went to classes, and received lessons in etiquette and manners and practical instruction in agriculture. After lunch, they returned to classes, followed by more prayers. The evening was spent in study and a final round of prayers before bed. By designing a curriculum that emphasized classical learning, deportment, and Christianity, Wheelock sought nothing less than to completely transform his charges from "heathens" and "savages" into Englishmen. Not surprisingly, results often fell short of these unrealistic and ethnocentric goals. Few of his pupils saw the advantage of adopting English ways, and, even if they did, Anglo-American society afforded precious few opportunities for Aboriginal men and women, however good their education. Many disheartened students left school early. Never questioning his own goals and methods, Wheelock blamed these failures on the students. He hoped that the Mohawks would prove more tractable.

Brant, at least, met Wheelock's every expectation. In letters to Johnson and others, the minister extolled the Mohawk's studiousness and character. In November, the minister praised Brant as "a considerate, Modest, and manly spirited youth. I am much pleased with him." In another letter, he spoke of Brant as possessing "a Sprightly Genius, a manly and genteel Deportment, and … a Modest courteous and benevolent Temper." Not only had Brant made great strides in reading and writing English, but Wheelock believed that he had undergone a conversion experience. Doubtless, Wheelock admired Brant's abilities, but his lavish, almost excessive, praise seems calculated to please Johnson, whose good opinion was necessary to obtain more Mohawk students. Not wishing to offend an important patron, Wheelock also spared his most important student the harsh treatments meted out to other pupils and ensured the boy had new clothes.

While Brant flourished under Wheelock's careful attention, Sander and Nickus withered. Sander had not recovered from his illness, and in October he returned to Canajoharie under Nickus's care. Neither boy returned to school. Sander succumbed to his illness and Nickus married. Brant, too, returned home in early November to visit his family and to find two recruits. Kirkland came with him in order to practice his Mohawk. Within the month, Brant and Kirkland had returned to Connecticut with two likely students, Moses and Johannes. Despite their youth, they too were veterans of the Seven Years War.

Brant continued to study under Wheelock for the next year and a half, until on May 15, 1763, a letter arrived

from Molly Brant ordering her brother to come home at once. The reason, Wheelock noted cryptically, was that "the Indians are displeased with his being … at school, that they don't like the People." Perhaps the Canajoharies did not like that Wheelock and his staff insisted men learn to farm. As women's work, fieldwork emasculated men. Brant would not have been the first Mohawk man to take up the plough, but critics may have feared that changes to the gender-based division of labour threatened the whole fabric of society. Perhaps also Molly Brant had heard rumours that the nations of the Northwest were then making preparations to drive the English off the continent, and she did not want her brother in the east, where he would be subject to a violent anti-Native backlash. Indeed, by the time Brant's letter reached Connecticut, the Ottawa warrior Pontiac and his followers had had Fort Detroit under siege for six days, and the war that would bear his name had spread. Brant remained at Wheelock's until July, and then dutifully packed his belongings and returned to live with his mother at Canajoharie.

Johnson considered placing Brant in a New York City school, but growing racial tensions that attended the continuation of Pontiac's War made the city a dangerous place for an Aboriginal man. Indeed, even Wheelock was not immune to the wild rumours spreading throughout the east. In March 1764, he inquired into the truthfulness of a charge that Brant had "put himself at the Head of a large party of Indians to fight against the English." Although the Reverend still felt kindly towards his protegé, he was motivated to write the letter for fear that funding for his school would dry up should it prove true.

Instead of returning to the east, Brant enrolled in a school operated at Canajoharie by Rev. Cornelius Bennet, a missionary for the Society for the Propagation of the Gospel, who had recently arrived in the Mohawk Valley. Brant studied with Bennet for a short while, but a warrior, however studious, could not long remain aloof from the conflict. War provided young men with opportunities to win reputations and influence, and Brant yielded to its temptations. Brant's formal education came to an end less

Pontiac Urges Warriors to Take Arms Against the British. *This drawing dates to the nineteenth century, as no contemporary images of Pontiac are known to exist.*

than four years after it began. Nevertheless, he had learned how to read and write English.

Pontiac's War had complex origins. The defeat of France in the Seven Years War had deprived First Peoples in the Ohio and Great Lakes regions of their French ally, leaving them dependent upon and vulnerable to Great Britain. At the same time, the French defeat emboldened Britain to act unilaterally with regards to the First Peoples. Commander-in-Chief General Jeffery Amherst, no friend of Native peoples, revamped Indian affairs in an effort to end what he believed was the misguided policy of "purchasing the good behaviour of Indians." Amherst forbade the customary practice of giving diplomatic presents and prohibited traders from providing gunpowder to hunters. In vain, Johnson protested measures that would make his job nearly impossible. First Peoples interpreted the stoppage of presents and powder as a hostile act, and soon communities experienced real deprivation, as hunters without ammunition could not harvest enough furs to supply their families' needs.

The withdrawal of presents underscored the dependence of First Peoples on European trade goods and fuelled a strain of militant theology that had surfaced among them in the 1730s. Increasingly, the middle decades of the eighteenth century witnessed the proliferation of prophets who sought to subsume distinct ethnic identities within a pan-Indian identity. Urging their people to reject European ways, these prophets taught that the Master of Life had created Europeans and Indians separately and provided them with different continents to live in. The mixture of the two races in America went against divine geography. The Delaware prophet Neolin, in particular, transformed separatist ideas into revolutionary action. Neolin, after prophesying that "Two or Three Good Talks" between Indians and Whites would be followed by war, endorsed armed resistance to further British encroachments.

Mohawks expressed no sympathy with Neolin's separatist theology. They had for too long enjoyed amicable relations with their German and Scot–Irish neighbours to find the arguments for militant nativism compelling. Moreover, Mohawk influence rose and fell with Britain's need for allies. While this attachment could and did generate tensions and resentments, it did not manifest in nativist sentiments. Indeed, as Pontiac's warriors sought to impose bloody separation between the races, bonds of necessity and sentiment compelled the Mohawks to embrace their English brethren and reject pan-Indianism. By the time Brant arrived home in July 1763, Pontiac's War had created near-panic in the Mohawk Valley. Frontier settlers deserted their farms for the safety of

Schenectady and Albany. At Sir William's newly completed manor house, Johnson Hall, Brant found his brother-in-law in bed sick, probably as a result of the wound he had received at Crown Point. Even in his weakened conditioned, Johnson had fortified his estate and had called council of the Six Nations to be held at German Flats in the western Mohawk Valley. The council convened that month with all of the nations in attendance except the Seneca who had taken up arms against the British.

Throughout the summer and fall, Brant travelled the length and breadth of the Mohawk Valley carrying messages to and from Johnson. In February, Brant became more actively involved in the conflict. Once again he took up his musket to join Mohawk and Oneida warriors for an expedition against the Delaware. Three Indian Department officers led the party first to the Oneida village of Kanowalohale, where more warriors joined the expedition, and then to Oquaga, another Oneida town on the Susquehanna River.

The expedition halted as Oquaga warriors prepared themselves for the coming campaign. The interval allowed Brant to see the town and to socialize with some of its residents. Perhaps Brant's own interest in Christianity drew him to Isaac, one of the village headmen who also served as a preacher. During visits to Isaac's house, Brant undoubtedly would have met Isaac's daughter and his future wife, Neggen.

On March 21, Oquaga warriors signalled their readiness. Brant shouldered his musket, bade farewell to Neggen, and marched towards Delaware country. The column trudged through wet, melting snow, forded rising creeks, and scoured the Susquehanna River for enemies. Despite signs of recent habitation, the countryside was deserted. Unable to strike the enemy, Brant and his fellow warriors put abandoned villages to the torch, destroying, according to one officer's reports, one hundred and thirty buildings, vast amounts of corn, and even the cattle that had been left behind. Plumes of smoke followed the warriors' destructive march through enemy territory.

By the fall of 1764, Pontiac's War had largely fizzled out.

A fanciful portrayal by a European artist of Pontiac leading warriors against the English in 1763.

First Peoples, dependent on Europeans for guns, ammunition, and other manufactured goods, could not sustain a prolonged conflict against the suppliers of those goods, at least not without the assistance of another European power. Smallpox also ravaged Native villages, further sapping the will of warriors to resist. The British may have been the cause of the outbreak, as they intentionally gave two blankets and a handkerchief from the smallpox hospital at Fort Pitt to some unsuspecting Delawares. Beset by internal differences, the western Seneca abandoned the effort and sued for peace. By the fall, warriors and British armies had fought to a standstill in the Ohio. With neither side able to

This print by Benjamin West, illustrating Colonel Henry Bouquet, an English officer, negotiating peace with a coalition of Delaware, Mingo and Shawnee tribes at the end of the French Indian War in 1764 in Ohio, captures the essence of a council meeting.

gain an advantage, a series of treaties in 1764–1765 restored the status quo.

Despite the lack of a clear-cut victory, the war did change things. Pontiac's War inaugurated a new kind of war, one premised on innate biological differences and one whose proponents aimed to violently enforce racial separation. In western Pennsylvania, attacks against British posts prompted swift reprisal. In December 1763, a mob murdered nearby Christian Conestogas who had had no part in the conflict. Although the "Paxton Massacre" occurred too late in the war to influence the British response, King

George III issued the Royal Proclamation of 1763, forbidding settlers to cross an invisible line drawn down the spine of the Appalachian Mountains, to lessen frontier tensions. Separating land-grasping colonists and First Nations, officials naively reasoned, would bring peace to America.

The Mohawk Valley had mercifully escaped the violence of Pontiac's War and the Paxton Massacre, but these events had deeply unsettled the region's population. Could their own long history of multiculturalism withstand the polarizing forces unleashed in 1763? Recent land frauds revealed deep cracks in the community's foundation. In 1761, a Palatine fur trader named George Klock had obtained a dubious patent to the planting lands around Canajoharie. What appeared on the surface to be a Mohawk–settler conflict, however, was much more complicated. As many as twenty Canajoharies supported Klock, while William Johnson and many Palatines, fearing the dispute would divide the neighbourhood, assisted the Mohawks. The Mohawks' allies included German families who had for many years rented farms from the Canajoharies. Ironically, Klock had arranged these lease agreements many years before, and now he threatened to evict the tenants if they did not leave voluntarily.

As disputes between Mohawks and settlers expanded, so too did opportunities for men like Brant to exercise leadership. Rather than return to Bennet's mission school, which in any case would close down when a smallpox outbreak struck the valley in 1765, Brant resolved to remain in his mother's home and oppose Klock and men of his ilk. In the early winter of 1765, Hance Tekarihogen, the head sachem of the Mohawks, and another man who appears in the documents only as Joseph, and probably was Joseph Brant, apprehended Cobus Maybe while he was in the process of persuading a few "beastly drunk" Canajoharies to sign a deed surrendering more lands. Maybe had already enraged the Mohawks by building a house on disputed lands. Before returning to Canajoharie, Tekarihogen

Built in 1750 by Johannes Klock, the brother of George Klock, Fort Klock's sturdy stone walls housed a fur trade post and served as a fort during the Seven Years War and the American Revolution.

demanded that Maybe vacate the lands. Maybe threatened to set fire to Canajoharie, but the warriors struck first, burning his house to the ground. Maybe defiantly rebuilt, ensuring the vexing dispute would continue to worry the Mohawks and divide the neighbourhood.

As Brant assumed a more public role, he also took on the responsibilities of a family. On July 22, 1765, at twenty-three years of age, Brant married Neggen at Canajoharie. Rev. Theophilas Chamberlain, a missionary recently sent to Canajoharie by Wheelock, presided over the ceremony, which included two other couples, including Brant Kaghneghtago, William Johnson's son by an unknown Mohawk woman, who married a war captive.

Marriage signified Joseph Brant's entrance into manhood at a time when he was assuming greater responsibility in the affairs of his people.

After Chamberlain declared Brant and Neggen husband and wife, guests gorged themselves on a wedding feast consisting of an ox, corn, and seven or eight kegs of alcohol. Chamberlain later learned that, in the ensuing drunkenness, two guests were stabbed. The significance was not that Brant had permitted his guests to lose control, but that by hosting the feast on a grand scale, he had demonstrated he could provide not only for his new family but also for young warriors who might one day follow him in war or against the likes of George Klock and Cobus Maybe.

CHAPTER 3
THE WHIRLWIND

The Haudenosaunee refer to the American Revolution as "the Whirlwind," a force so destructive that it destroyed the Confederacy and scattered its people widely. Unlike natural disasters, however, human minds and hands directed the Revolution. Two of the strongest proponents of Haudenosaunee participation in the war were Joseph and Molly Brant. Their wartime careers reveal how actions may have unforeseen consequences. By encouraging the Six Nations to join the British against the rebellious colonists as the best means of preserving their homeland, they helped bring about the destruction of the multicultural communities they had inhabited and became exiles in a foreign land.

In 1765, the same year colonists on the eastern seaboard rioted to protest the Stamp Act, Brant and his new wife, Neggen, went to Oswego, where for several months he served as an interpreter. There, Neggen gave birth to a son whom they named Isaac after her father. On returning to the Mohawk Valley, the young family lived with Brant's

Indian Castle Church, Mohawk Valley, New York. Built in 1769 by William Johnson for the use of the Canajoharie Mohawks, this restored church is the only building associated with the Canajoharie Mohawks that still stands.

mother, Margaret, who was probably a widow again, as Kanagaradunckwa had disappeared from the records. Brant owned eighty acres around the house, although it is not clear who worked the land. Women were the traditional farmers in Mohawk society, but Brant had received agricultural instruction at Wheelock's. Increasingly, individuals like Brant were transforming communal land into private farms. Perhaps they had absorbed European notions of private property or perhaps they found well-defined, individually owned lots easier to defend against men like George Klock. In addition to the farm, Brant occasionally worked for the Indian Department, served as a guide, and possibly operated a store. In 1769, Brant and Neggen had their second child, a daughter named Christina. Neggen, however, had contracted tuberculosis and died in early 1771.

In the spring of 1772, Brant moved temporarily to Tiononderoge to assist the Anglican minister who had been installed at Queen Anne's Chapel two years earlier. The new man, Rev. John Stuart, required a reliable interpreter to translate his sermons into Mohawk, and the grieving widower readily agreed. In addition to his interpreting duties, Brant also assisted Stuart in translating the Gospel of St. Mark and some other works into Mohawk, a task that would occupy his time intermittently for the next two years. During the collaboration, the two men became fast friends. Brant, therefore, must have been disappointed when Stuart, repulsed by the Haudenosaunee custom of a widower marrying his sister-in-law, refused his friend's request to marry him to Susanna, Neggen's sister. Brant eventually found another minister who would perform the ceremony.

Brant's turbulent private life reflected the confusion at Canajoharie. The unresolved dispute with George Klock assumed a new dimension at the end of 1773, when Klock, accompanied by at least two Mohawks, set sail for England aboard a ship ironically named the *William Johnson*. Klock, unable to win community support in his dispute against the Mohawks, hoped to lay his grievances before the king. His reputation as a "notorious bad Character" preceded him, however, and the old German instead found himself running from the law. Thwarted, Klock returned

A Mohawk village in central New York, about 1780.

to the Mohawk Valley, only to have Brant, at the head of twenty warriors, arrive at his farm ostensibly to collect money Klock had stolen from one of his Mohawk travelling companions. The real reason for the visit, however, was to intimidate Klock into signing a release to the lands around Canajoharie. When Klock predictably refused, warriors ransacked his house. Later, Klock accused Brant of striking him with his own pistol, while four other warriors beat him into unconsciousness. A month later, Brant returned with thirty supporters. This time Klock spied the approaching Canajoharies and beat a hasty retreat. Finding the house empty, warriors cursed Klock and killed a number of his sheep.

In contrast to the Canajoharie land dispute, which had so far been contained, Shawnee attempts to protect their lands in what is present-day Kentucky threatened to embroil the colonies in a war. Warriors had been fighting intermittently with settlers since the close of the Seven Years War, but, as the conflict intensified, militants worked to rebuild a new confederacy to oppose further encroachments. In order to prevent a general frontier war, William Johnson convened a council at Johnson Hall in July 1774. Approximately six hundred Haudenosaunee delegates assembled to listen as Warraghiyagey (Johnson) urged the

Rev. John Stuart, the Anglican minister to the Tiononderoge Mohawks who collaborated with Brant to translate the gospels.

Six Nations to remain at peace. When it was the Mohawks' turn to speak, Tekarihogen recounted the Canajoharies' troubles with George Klock. Citing Johnson's inability to settle the matter, the chief drew parallels between the plight of his own people and the Shawnee. Johnson furiously upbraided the Canajoharies for raising the issue. Then, exhausted, he retired to the house. Within the hour, he was dead.

Certainly, Joseph Brant must have joined the more than two thousand people who turned out to lament Johnson's passing. Mourners escorted the body from Johnson Hall to St. John's Anglican Church in Johnstown. Fittingly, the baronet would be laid to rest in a town he had established on his own lands and with his own money to be the seat of Tryon County, a county he had created two years earlier. The Reverend John Stuart led the procession, followed by the coffin. Johnson's son and heir, Sir John Johnson, and his sons-in-law, Guy Johnson and Daniel Claus, took their places behind the casket. Next came the physicians and family members. Significantly, the Canajoharies and Tiononderoges occupied a prominent position immediately behind the family and ahead of Johnson's friends, neighbours, and tenants. The remainder of the Six Nations brought up the rear. At the church, Stuart read the services.

The day after the public funeral, Molly and Joseph would have attended a Haudenosaunee ceremony to perform the Condolence ritual. All of the Six Nations acknowledged the Mohawks had lost a friend and kinsman in Johnson. Accordingly, they condoled their brothers' grief and then, as was customary upon the death of one chief, raised another to replace him. In this case, they selected Guy Johnson, whom they addressed as Uraghquadirha, to replace Warraghiyagey.

No one person could replace William Johnson. His son, Sir John Johnson, took no interest in politics or Indian affairs. Having inherited Johnson Hall, he wished only to remain quietly upon his estate. Unable or unwilling to share her home with John Johnson and his wife, Mary Watts Johnson, Molly Brant returned to Canajoharie, where she and her eight children crowded into Margaret's house with Joseph's family. Daniel Claus was spending much of his time in Montreal, where he had served as deputy superintendent since the conquest. That left the leadership of the Johnson family to Guy Johnson, whose talents did not match his ambitions. He was ill-prepared to resist the coming storm.

In the summer of 1774, colonial protests against British measures reached new levels of intensity. Parliament had recently passed a series of draconian acts intended to punish the people of Massachusetts for their part in the Boston Tea Party in December of the previous year. Colonists responded to the so-called Intolerable Acts by appointing a Continental Congress to organize a

Council Fire at Johnson Hall, *painted in 1903 by Edward Lamson Henry, depicts Johnson Hall as a diplomatic hub.*

boycott of British goods. These far-away events would have momentous consequences for the Mohawks.

Until this time, the people of the Mohawk Valley had paid scant attention to the imperial crisis. Johnson's death, however, left a vacuum that ambitious men sought to fill. On August 27, 1774, a group of men gathered at Adam Loucks's tavern north of the Mohawk River to discuss deteriorating relations between the colonies and Britain. After condemning Parliament's recent "oppressive" and "arbitrary" actions, the attendees established a Committee of Safety to bring the region into compliance with Congress's decrees. The committee posed a direct challenge to the authority of the Johnson family, whose members and supporters effectively governed Tryon County. During the second meeting, the committee more precisely articulated their grievances when they claimed "This County has for a series of Years been ruled by one family, the different Branches of which are still strenuous in dissuading people from coming into Congressional Measures." Local Whigs were taking advantage of Sir William's death to deprive his heirs of power.

A Tory by inclination, Guy Johnson despised the committeemen and everything they stood for. Rather than confront the weakly organized committee, he succumbed to paranoia and self-doubt and barricaded himself inside his mansion, Guy Park, posting tenants to guard the house. Johnson even imprisoned Brant's old friend Samuel Kirkland, who had, as minister to the Oneidas, promoted the Whig cause in those quarters. Johnson's bizarre behaviour alarmed neighbours and permitted the

Built by Guy Johnson in 1774, Guy Park replaced an earlier home that had been destroyed by lightning. The state confiscated the property when Johnson fled Tryon County at the outbreak of the American Revolution.

Whigs to expand and consolidate their hold on the county.

It is not clear how Joseph Brant interpreted these events. Probably, he was more focused on the ongoing land dispute with Klock and did not fully comprehend that one of his most important allies was becoming marginalized. Just a week after the formation of the Committee of Safety, Mohawk and Palatine residents of the Canajoharie neighbourhood met publicly to discuss not politics but what to do about Klock. Canajoharies asked their neighbours for help, and the Palatines agreed to circulate a petition condemning Klock's actions. Klock did not stand idly by. In a letter to the governor, he cast the proceedings in a more sinister light. He charged Brant of conspiring with his Palatine neighbours, most notably the assemblyman and militia colonel Hendrick Frey, to have him killed. There the record of the Klock dispute ends, as the revolution's outbreak in the Mohawk Valley swept away all other issues.

In May 1775, a little over a month after the first shots of the revolution were fired at Lexington and Concord, Brant accompanied Johnson as he left the protection of Guy Park to hold a council with the Six Nations at the German Flats. With him went Daniel Claus and John Butler, along with his family, ninety Mohawks, and 120 tenants and other supporters. Travelling through the countryside, Johnson experienced first hand the fear and hostility many local residents felt towards him. After the meeting, Johnson continued with his followers, Brant included, into Canada rather than return to face hostile neighbours. The decision to leave the Mohawk Valley was personally costly. Brant left behind Susanna and his children, Isaac and Christina. Although Johnson abandoned a valuable estate, he decided to take his wife, Mary, and his daughter with him into exile. Sadly, Mary died before they reached Montreal.

Arriving in Montreal in the middle of July, Johnson and Claus were met not as loyal heroes but with thinly veiled disdain. Governor Guy Carleton disliked the Johnson clan intensely for the little empire Sir William had carefully cultivated and because he opposed Guy Johnson's plans for employing warriors against the colonies. The governor worried that "the innocent might have suffered with the guilty" in a frontier war. Johnson's position became more tenuous in the fall, when Major John Campbell arrived from England with orders to take charge of Indian affairs in Quebec. Campbell's appointment put Daniel Claus out of a job and threatened to break the Johnson family's grip on the Indian Department. Determined to take their case to the highest levels, on November 11, 1775, Johnson, Claus, and a retinue of close associates boarded a ship bound for England.

Brant also made the trip to England. He sought neither patronage nor favours. Rather, he wanted assurances that imperial authorities would address long-standing Mohawk grievances. Brant was a hit in London. The arrival of a Mohawk "chief" at a time when armed conflict in America seemed likely generated considerable curiosity. Gentlemen sought his company and pressed him with gifts and party invitations. The Earl of Warwick paid to have Brant's portrait done by English painter George Romney. A local lodge even inducted him into the mysteries of Freemasonry.

Brant did not allow the attractions of London to divert him from seeking out the nation's leaders. Although he had an audience with the king, Brant's most important meetings took place with the colonial secretary, Lord George Germain. Germain lacked Carleton's squeamish-

Joseph Brant as painted by George Romney.

ness about employing warriors against the rebels, and he was delighted to talk with Brant. Doubtless, Germain overestimated Brant's influence with the Six Nations, a notion Brant did nothing to correct. Brant laid bare Mohawk complaints and Britain's backwardness in dealing with its allies. Loyalty to Britain during the last two wars had cost many Mohawk lives, yet Britain had done nothing to protect Mohawk lands. Germain gave assurances that he would address the Mohawks' land disputes, but only after the present troubles in America had been settled. In effect, the British government would assist the Mohawks only once the Mohawks had aided in crushing the rebellion.

Guy Johnson, too, got what he wanted, confirmation of his command over the Indian Department. It was Johnson's influence with the Six Nations rather than his abilities that persuaded Germain to offer him the commission. Even though Claus had not been restored to his former position, the party embarked for British-held New York in early June 1776. The return voyage was dangerous. American privateers prowled the oceans in search of lightly armed British vessels, and one of these attacked Brant's ship. While the crew tried to fend off the attackers with cannon, Brant and another Mohawk sniped at American officers with rifles they had received as gifts in London. Eventually, the British ship broke away from its pursuer and limped into New York City in late July.

The military situation forced Brant to remain in New York City for the rest of the summer. By fall, he had become impatient to return home and relay news of his meeting with Germain. Johnson, however, showed no indication that he was ready to leave the comforts of the city for the upper country. Determined to go alone if he must, Brant received permission from Commander-in-Chief William Howe to take his friend Captain Gilbert Tice and strike out overland in November. Donning disguises, the two men travelled at night until they reached his father-in-law's village, Oquaga. Brant tried to rally support for the British cause, but Oquaga, like most villages, was deeply divided and was trying to remain neutral in what they considered to be an unnatural war between the king and his American children.

Leaving Oquaga, Brant and Tice visited Delaware and Seneca villages, where they met some success, before stopping at Fort Niagara, where John Butler had command of the Indian Department in Johnson's absence. Brant thought Butler treated him coolly. Daniel Claus dismissed Butler's reaction as "jealousy and envy." Butler, however, was still under Carleton's orders to restrain the warriors, and Brant's zealous recruiting threatened to unleash a frontier war. Unwilling to waste a moment of time, Brant trudged in the winter snows through the nations of the Longhouse rallying support for the British cause. The final meeting took place with the Oneida and Tuscarora, who rejected his entreaties. Unable to do more, Brant spent the winter at Cayuga.

Butler need not have worried. While most villages gave Brant a friendly reception, the exhortations of a young warrior could not have persuaded chiefs and headmen to abandon neutrality. Indeed, most of the Six Nations remained uncommitted until July 1777, when, at a council hosted by Butler, they would fatefully promise to take up the British hatchet. Although the Mohawks played an important role at this meeting, Brant was not in attendance. Tuscaroras and Oneidas, Brant's in-laws included, broke with their brethren and sided with the Americans.

⋯⋅⋯

The following spring, Brant abandoned diplomacy for direct action. Scouring the mountainous regions of the Delaware and Susquehanna rivers recruiting soldiers, he soon had a party consisting of a few Mohawk and Oquaga warriors and seventy or eighty Loyalists. Calling themselves Brant's Volunteers, these men preferred to follow a Mohawk without pay or provisions rather than join one of the Loyalist units then forming in Canada. Although not drawn from the Mohawk Valley, Brant's war parties reflected the multi-ethnic composition of his homeland. The small number of warriors he attracted, however, suggests that his influence remained limited and his cause remained unpopular, even among Mohawks.

The Georgian-style home of General Nicholas Herkimer near Little Falls, New York.
Opposite: A button from a Butler's Rangers uniform; cannonballs dating from the American Revolution.

From his headquarters at the forks of the Susquehanna and Unadilla rivers, Brant continued to recruit Loyalist support during the early summer of 1777. Rebel sympathizers fled, spreading warnings of Brant's activities, and, in July, American Brigadier General Nicholas Herkimer led the Tryon County militia to Unadilla to speak with Brant. The two men had once been neighbours and friends, and Herkimer now urged Brant to stay neutral. Brant refused, and the discussions became heated when Colonel Ebenezer Cox, George Klock's son-in-law, insulted Brant. The warriors snatched up their guns, but the leaders managed to diffuse the situation. Brant then pushed Herkimer to attend to the needs of his friends and kinsmen still living on the Mohawk River. Herkimer agreed to allow the Tiononderoges to settle among the remaining

Canajoharies and to permit Rev. John Stuart and Mrs. Butler, who remained at home after her husband had left for Quebec, to visit Canajoharie. That Brant seemingly dictated terms chagrined Herkimer's superiors.

Brant then led approximately three hundred men to Oswego, where they joined General Barry St. Leger's British expedition against Fort Stanwix, which guarded the head of the Mohawk Valley. St. Leger's army was part of a three-pronged attack intended to seize New York and isolate New England. At Oswego, Brant met many friends and neighbours. John Johnson, who had fled the Mohawk Valley the previous May, was there commanding his own Loyalist regiment, the King's Royal Regiment of New York. John Butler was there also, in command of a Loyalist battalion, Butler's Rangers. Despite having persuaded the

A tavern near the Loyalist settlement of Niagara. The tavern was operated in this house by Gilbert Tice's widow. Tice, who had accompanied Brant from New York City to Iroquoia in 1776, died in 1791.

Six Nations to participate in the campaign, Butler was not in charge of the Indian Department. That task fell to Daniel Claus, who had wrangled a commission to oversee management of the Six Nations for the duration of the campaign.

On August 2, St. Leger's force arrived in front of Fort Stanwix. It fell to General Nicholas Herkimer to raise the Tryon County militia and march to the relief of the besieged defenders. The militia consisted primarily of Mohawk Valley Palatines. From her home at Canajoharie, Molly Brant observed Herkimer's preparations and sent warnings to the British of the militia's approach. Johnson, Butler, and Brant mustered the Loyalist soldiers and warriors and marched to the Oneida community of Oriska (in present-day Oneida County), where they prepared an ambush.

On the morning of August 6, over eight hundred militiamen and Oneida scouts marched into the carefully laid ambuscade. The forest in their front erupted in smoke and fire. Herkimer had his leg shattered by a musket ball and directed the battle from beneath a tree. Despite heavy losses, the militia stood their ground. After six hours of fighting, the warriors had had enough and retreated. The Loyalists soon followed. When the smoke cleared, two hundred and fifty militiamen lay dead and wounded. Fifty Loyalists were killed and wounded. The warriors sustained more than sixty casualties. The militia's failure to break the siege allowed St. Leger to claim victory, but the Six Nations considered the Battle of Oriskany, as it became known, a complete disaster.

Upon learning that an American force was on its way, St. Leger lifted the siege on August 22 and retreated. Before the army departed, warriors burned Oriska in retaliation for its assistance of the militia. A short while later, Oneida warriors and American militia sacked Canajoharie. The Oneidas vented their rage against the home of Molly Brant, since she had given the warning about Herkimer's relief party. Brant, however, had already escaped. Later the Oneidas handed out the same treatment to Tiononderoge. In the wake of these attacks, the remaining Canajoharies went to Niagara, and one hundred Tiononderoges fled to Montreal.

⁛

Haudenosaunee, stung by high casualties, must have questioned the wisdom of supporting the hapless British when they learned in October that British General John Burgoyne had surrendered his army at Saratoga. With the head war chief, Sayengaraghta, wavering, Molly Brant intervened to shore up support for the British war effort. She had been living with relatives at Cayuga after leaving Canajoharie. As a clan mother, she exerted considerable influence over the warriors. Weeping as she spoke, she implored Sayengaraghta to remember his friendship with Warraghiyagey and his commitments to the Crown. Moved by Brant's entreaties, Sayengaraghta reaffirmed his support for the war.

British officers took to heart Daniel Claus's claim that "one word from [Molly Brant] is more taken notice of by the five Nations than a thousand from a white man without exception." The military and Indian Department so valued Brant's abilities and influence with warriors that they underwrote her diplomacy with lavish material support. Brant appears to have had free access to military stores, and took whatever she desired. Having to please such a strong and confident woman frightened many post commanders, and most were relieved when she moved on to continue her work at some other fort. Therefore, Colonel Mason Bolton, the commander of Fort Niagara, must have cursed when he discovered in 1778 that Butler had persuaded Brant to relocate to his post, where her services would be of more value.

Brant remained at Niagara with her children until the summer of 1779. By then, Niagara had become so crowded with refugees and prisoners that Bolton thought Brant should transfer to Montreal. Bolton, who found Brant demanding and hot-tempered, may have suggested the move simply to be rid of her. After a brief sojourn in

Major John Butler.

Montreal, she settled at the British fort on Carleton Island in the St. Lawrence River, where she continued to promote the British cause.

As Molly Brant was emerging as an important force in Haudenosaunee politics, her brother Joseph was beginning to gain a reputation as an able warrior. In May 1778, Brant, with three hundred men, had ambushed a group of about fifty regulars and militia near Cobbleskill in the Schoharie Valley. After a sharp fight in which nearly twenty of the Americans were killed — five perished when the house they were in was set on fire — Brant destroyed all of the homes and barns in the area and killed whatever cattle he could not carry off.

So ferocious was Brant's reputation among his opponents that Americans incorrectly credited him almost any

The Swiss-born Frederick Haldimand served as commander-in-chief of British forces in North America and became one of Brant's highly placed allies.

Opposite: Soldiers in Butler's Rangers wore brass plates like this one, ca. 1777, on their cartridge box slings to identify their regiments.

frontier raid. It was widely believed that Brant had taken a leading part in killing civilians at the so-called Wyoming Massacre in June, even though he was not present at the battle. Thereafter, his enemies feared and despised the "monster Brant."

In September, with over four hundred warriors and his Volunteers, Brant struck the Palatine village of German Flats, destroying more than a hundred houses and barns and several mills. Only four buildings remained intact, a church, the fort, which he tried to capture without success, and two houses belonging to Loyalists. Two months later, Brant's force had shrunk to eighty Loyalists and "a few Indians." With these, he joined forces with John Butler's son, Captain Walter Butler, in November to attack Cherry Valley, on a branch of the Susquehanna River very near the Mohawk Valley. The two men disliked each other. The younger Butler's arrogance so irritated Brant that he considered quitting the expedition. Warriors, however, prevailed on him to stay.

When the attack began, Seneca warriors descended on the community, killing indiscriminately. Several Loyalists were killed, including Robert Wells and his family. Wells had been a supporter of William Johnson and a good friend of Brant. In total, more than thirty civilians died in the attack. Americans decried the Cherry Valley Massacre and denounced the perpetrators as savages. Many British officers also felt squeamish about the way First Peoples and Loyalists conducted warfare. Claus and Colonel Mason Bolton, the commander at Niagara, attempted to distance Brant from the affair, assuring Commander-in-Chief Sir Frederick Haldimand at Quebec that he had treated all prisoners "with great humanity."

Susanna likely died that fall or winter. A widower once again, Brant sent his children, Isaac and Christina, to live in Iroquoia, rather than expose them to the unhealthy conditions and crudities of a military post. Instead of joining his family once the onset of winter brought a halt to active campaigning, Brant set out for Quebec. He wanted to remind Haldimand of British promises to the Mohawks. Brant's charm and social graces soon won over the general. Despite receiving favourable reports about Brant from Claus and Bolton, Haldimand, like most British officers, had expected Native people to behave like savages. To the general's ethnocentric eyes, however, the educated and affable Brant seemed to transcend the limitations of his people. Brant left Quebec with a captain's salary for himself, guaranteed assistance for Molly Brant, and the promise of land for the Mohawks should they be prevented from returning home after the war.

The two men gravitated to each other for different reasons, but their goals were not necessarily contradictory. Haldimand hoped that Brant, given the proper resources, could bolster support for the war among the Six Nations and exert a moderating and "civilizing" influence on the warriors. Brant, for his part, saw Haldimand as a replacement for William Johnson, a highly placed source of goods and prestige through which he could enlarge his own following in order to achieve Mohawk ends. The first material signs of this new alliance appeared in the spring of 1779. Haldimand ordered Colonel Bolton to supply Brant with clothes and blankets for his supporters.

·:·:·

In a little more than a year, Brant, Sayengaraghta, and the Butlers had devastated large swaths of western New York and Pennsylvania. Frightened survivors abandoned one of the most productive agricultural regions. Unable to ignore this threat to the northern frontier, George Washington authorized General John Sullivan to invade Iroquoia and to systematically destroy Haudenosaunee villages. Sullivan set his 4,500-strong army in motion in mid-June, and for the next month and a half, marched virtually unopposed through Cayuga and Seneca country. Families fled before the advancing Americans, while Butler's Rangers and warriors harassed but could not stop the army. Soldiers burned anything and everything of value. Flames consumed forty villages and 160,000 bushels of corn. After the war, unemployed veterans of the campaign, recalling the rich soils, luxuriant cornfields, and full storehouses of Iroquoia, would form the vanguard of a settler invasion. Brant, whose little force shadowed the massive army, seems to have understood the short- and long-term significance of the Sullivan expedition. To Claus he wrote, "[W]e shall begin to know what is to befal us the People of the Long House."

The final act of the Sullivan campaign occurred on September 29, when Colonel Peter Gansevoort's regiment, returning from Iroquoia, marched into Tion, onderoge. At the time, only four houses were occupied, as most of the inhabitants had gone to Canada. Gansevoort evicted the remaining Mohawks and allowed local settlers to occupy the village.

For Washington's part in ordering the destruction of Six Nations' villages, the Haudenosaunee called him "Town Destroyer." Indeed, Sullivan's army had unleashed the Whirlwind that made the Haudenosaunee a refugee people. Upwards of five thousand Onondagas, Senecas, Cayugas, and Mohawks converged on Niagara. The sudden appearance of so many people lacking even the barest necessities staggered the British commissary. Guy Johnson, who had arrived at the post just in time to deal with the crisis, could not adequately care for the multitude. Competing demands made a difficult job impossible. On one side, destitute Haudenosaunee demanded vast quantities of food, clothing, and shelter. Johnson could hardly say no without alienating the very warriors and chiefs on whom the British war effort depended. On the other hand, Haldimand, alarmed at the rising costs of Indian affairs, preached economy and thrift. Eventually refugees found temporary homes in huts and tents that formed a line of settlement stretching from present-day Lewiston to Buffalo. Nevertheless, many died of starvation and exposure in the harsh winter that followed.

In these bleak, makeshift quarters, Brant married for the third and final time. His bride, Adonwentishon, also known as Catharine Croghan, was the daughter of Irish fur trader and Indian agent George Croghan and a Mohawk mother. The union distanced Brant from his pro-American Oneida in-laws and cemented an old alliance. Adonwentishon was also the niece of Tekarihogen, the Mohawks' head sachem and Brant's old ally against George Klock. Like Molly Brant, Adonwentishon was one of the powerful clan mothers. Each within their own spheres of influence — Brant the warrior, Adonwentishon the clan mother, and Tekarihogen the chief — would reinforce each other's authority and exert a powerful influence over the Haudenosaunee at their moment of crisis.

That winter, Johnson divided the refugees into seven companies and placed each under the management of an Indian Department officer. Brant took charge of nearly 450 people, predominantly Mohawks, living near Niagara. Befitting his new responsibilities, Brant also received the rank of captain. Lord George Germain had issued Brant a colonel's commission. Haldimand, however, withheld the promotion, believing that the Haudenosaunee did not consider Brant among their best warriors and to elevate him above Sayengaraghta and others would excite jealousies and disagreements. Haldimand was right. However much Brant had enhanced his reputation and status on the battlefield and through skilful marriage alliances, he was still one of many notable warriors.

Like any warrior, Brant had to keep his followers provisioned or risk losing them to a more capable and generous leader. As the number of Brant's followers increased, so too did his demands on the Indian Department stores. Under orders to reduce costs, officers complained that Brant was "more difficult to please than any of the other Chiefs." Haldimand, who constantly lectured Johnson on economy, exacerbated the situation by insisting that exceptions be made for Brant. The demands of Haudenosaunee leadership, dependent as it was on reciprocity, brought Brant into conflict with the very friends that had assisted his rise to power. Growing tensions led Brant to quarrel with both Johnson and Butler and brawl with an Indian Department employee.

Throughout 1780, Brant continued to raid settlements on the Mohawk and Susquehanna rivers. After attacking Schoharie and Harpersfield in the early spring, his men burned an Oneida town in retaliation for the Oneidas driving Mohawks from their villages. In August, he joined Johnson's King's Royal Regiment of New York for a raid against the Mohawk Valley. Two hundred homes and 150,000 bushels of wheat went up in flames.

The next year, Brant left Niagara for Detroit. Ostensibly, Brant and seventeen warriors went west to assist in repelling George Rogers Clark's invasion of the Ohio country, Brant's birthplace, but the reason for his departure probably had as much to do with his deteriorating relations with the Indian Department as the military situation. Nevertheless, Brant made a good account of himself. Ambushing an American relief column, he and his men killed and captured a hundred men.

When Brant returned to Niagara in the spring of 1782, a gloom hung over the place. Guy Johnson was in Montreal answering charges of corruption within the Indian Department. He had run the department as Sir William had, and his guilt lay primarily in not sensing the shift in British policy toward economy and strict accountability. Rumours drifted northward that Lord Cornwallis had surrendered his army at a place called Yorktown. Under a cloud, Brant gathered three hundred warriors and a handful of his Volunteers and went to help fortify Oswego.

In July, Brant left Oswego for the Mohawk Valley with a large war party. Virtually nothing remained to destroy. After killing eight or nine men and capturing some cattle, he received orders to return to Oswego. A temporary cessation of hostilities had been announced. The warrior Brant had fought his last battle. With the return of peace, he would refashion himself as a diplomat.

Uniform of Lieutenant Jeremiah French, 2nd Battalion, King's Royal Regiment of New York (John Johnson's regiment).

CHAPTER 4
ALLIANCES

News of the preliminary treaty of peace reached Niagara in May 1783, confirming what most already suspected: Britain had capitulated to the United States. When Joseph Brant learned the details, he exploded that "England had sold the Indians to Congress." Indeed, Britain had betrayed its allies not once but twice. First, negotiators had failed either to protect or to even mention the First Nations within the body of the text. Not only did Iroquoia fall within the boundaries of the new United States, but the Haudenosaunee, like other First Peoples, would also have to negotiate a separate peace with the Americans. Second, British officials in North America tried unsuccessfully to keep the terms of the treaty secret for fear that, once revealed, they would spark a second Pontiac's War.

Brant immediately left for Quebec to query General Frederick Haldimand about the treaty and remind him of his and Lord Germain's earlier promises to the Mohawks. Haldimand could provide no definite answers, in part because he knew little more than Brant, but he did take concrete steps to assuage Brant and the Mohawks. The general proposed resettling the Mohawks in Quebec. Brant agreed to the idea and accompanied a surveyor to scout suitable locations in the region around Cataraqui, present-day Kingston. In time, Haldimand would also agree to build a sawmill, a gristmill, a church, and a school, and to support the Mohawks' application for compensation for wartime losses. To appease other First Nations, Haldimand broke the terms of the peace by ordering the retention of British-occupied forts on what was now the United States' side of the border.

Portrait of Joseph Brant, about 1785.

Top: The Loyalists had not yet settled Niagara when Henry Fuseli painted this scene, about 1770.
Below: The head of Lake Ontario, watercolour over pencil, 1796, by Elizabeth Simcoe (1766–1850)

Brant had undertaken earlier diplomatic missions to London and Quebec, but these negotiations over a new Mohawk homeland marked his emergence as a civil leader of considerable consequence. He was no longer just a promising young warrior. His battlefield successes, popularity with warriors, and influence with British officials made him a mature and potent force within Haudenosaunee politics. Obtaining a new homeland for the Mohawks and others of the Six Nations who wished to reside in British North America provided further evidence of Brant's leadership qualities. But though Brant grew into the role of spokesperson and representative of the Six Nations, he continued to view the world as a Canajoharie Mohawk.

Soon after Brant's departure for Quebec, the commander of Fort Niagara reported that the Haudenosaunee might take revenge for the peace treaty by attacking the post. Haldimand called on John Johnson, Guy Johnson's replacement as superintendent in the Indian Department, to go to Niagara and soothe the Six Nations. After an unconscionable delay of nearly two months, Johnson finally arrived to a rough reception, as headmen lectured him on British duplicity. Nevertheless, the new superintendent

Encampment of the Loyalists at Johnstown (Cornwall), June 6, 1784. Similar conditions would have prevailed at Niagara until the Loyalists could be given land and tools to begin the task of resettlement. Right: Cup of Indian Department officer Daniel Servos, who settled in the Niagara area.

propagated the fictions that First Peoples' lands were secure and that the king would protect them. Brant, who had returned to Niagara, could listen patiently to his kinsman's bland pronouncements, knowing that he had already secured a new homeland for the Mohawks.

Brant's work was far from done, however. Throughout the 1780s and early 1790s, he confronted three critical issues. A new settlement had to be laid out. Peace terms had to be negotiated with the United States. A confederacy of First Nations, preferably under Mohawk leadership, had to be created in order to present a united front to the Americans during negotiations.

The first of these problems, the new settlement, appeared to have been solved, as Brant and the surveyor had identified a location at the Bay of Quinte, west of Cataraqui. Upon further reflection, however, Brant

declared Quinte ill-suited to his purposes. The site was too far from the Senecas, who had removed to Buffalo Creek, the site of modern-day Buffalo, New York, the Loyalist soldiers then settling at Niagara, and from the nations of the Ohio. Not wanting to be isolated, he proposed another location on the Ouse — or Grand — River, west of Lake Ontario. The Grand River offered several advantages. It was near major population centres and transportation routes and possessed fertile soils and a mild climate. Although Haldimand would have preferred the Mohawks to settle at Quinte, where they would be more susceptible to British influence, he dared not alienate Brant at such a critical juncture. Accordingly, he instructed John Johnson to purchase the Grand River from its original owners, the Mississaugas. In May 1784, the Mississaugas parted with

The first Anglican church in what is now Ontario, St. Paul's, was built by the Crown for the Mohawks in 1785. It is now known as the Mohawk Chapel.
Left: A Bible belonging to the Nelles family, now in the Grimsby Museum.

Six Nations, along with a number of Tutelos, Delawares, and Nanticokes, went to the Grand River. Each group settled in separate ethnically distinct villages. The Cayugas occupied land near the mouth of the Grand River opposite a small Seneca community, while the Mohawks established a village on a bend halfway up the river. Settling together on the same tract, albeit in separate towns, had certain advantages. Individual villages preserved local autonomy and cultural distinctiveness, while collectively, the Grand River's inhabitants wielded more political and military clout than if they had settled separately.

Not all Haudenosaunee settled at Grand River. The majority, approximately two-thirds, returned to their homes or established new communities in what would become western New York. The most important of these, the Seneca-dominated community of Buffalo Creek, became the political and spiritual centre of the New York Haudenosaunee and rivalled Grand River in importance. Nor were the Mohawks unanimous in their desire to live at Grand River. Approximately half of the Tiononderoge Mohawks decided to live at the Bay of Quinte, where they would be farther from the United States and could preserve their independence from the Canajoharie Mohawks. However, three Tiononderoge Mohawks of note, David Hill, Isaac Hill, and Aaron Hill (despite sharing the same last name, the relationship between these men is uncertain) and their supporters, followed their friend Brant to the new location. Disappointed that the settlement did not attract more people, Brant would work for the remainder of his life to unite the Haudenosaunee at Grand River.

The Mohawk Village, also called Brant's Town, became the political centre of the new settlement. Situated on a rise overlooking the river and near a ford that bears Brant's name, the town consisted mostly of two-room log homes. A cluster of buildings formed the focal point of the community. The largest and most imposing structure was St. Paul's, a clapboarded log church measuring sixty feet by forty-five feet that came to be known as the Mohawk Chapel. A steeple containing a bell rose impressively from the roofline, while the inside of the church was furnished with a pulpit,

about 570,000 acres extending six miles on either side of the Grand River from its mouth to its source.

Between the fall of 1784 and the spring of 1785, refugee communities along the Niagara River gradually broke up, as families ferried their meagre possessions across the river and made the short journey to their new homes. In total, more than eighteen hundred people, representing all of the reading desk, communion table, pews, an organ, and a partial set of communion silver. John Stuart had rescued the silverware from Queen Anne's Chapel at Fort Hunter and delivered half to the Bay of Quinte Mohawks and half to Grand River. The Mohawks shared a minister, just one of three Anglican clergymen in the entire colony, with Niagara. While the minister arrived occasionally to perform baptisms, a Mohawk usually read services. Nearby was a solid log schoolhouse that doubled as a meeting-house until 1793, when the Mohawks prevailed on the lieutenant-governor to build a council house. South of the church stood an impressive two-storey, frame house belonging to Joseph Brant. On the river, a government-built gristmill served the town and surrounding countryside.

A white fence and a British flag flying in the yard set Brant's house off from the rest of the community, while chinaware, fine furniture, English sheets, and a well-stocked liquor cabinet marked the occupants as people of distinction. Brant entertained often and lavishly. At one time or another, chiefs, ministers, government officials, military men, and the lieutenant-governor all enjoyed Brant's hospitality. Some have compared the Brant household to a miniature Johnson Hall and Brant to an aspiring William Johnson. Certainly, in Catharine, Brant had a partner whose abilities and influence complemented his own, just as Molly Brant and Johnson had reinforced one another's power. Doubtless, Brant did emulate his late patron and brother-in-law, but hospitality had always been

Children attending school at the Mohawk Village in 1786. The teacher is probably Paulus, Hendrick's son.

integral to Haudenosaunee society and politics. That Brant served tea in china cups mattered less than the fact that he shared what he had and, as result, he often complained of having no money. The picket fence and luxurious furnishings did not segregate Brant from other Mohawks so much as remind people of both his success

The Mohawk Village as it appeared in 1793. The building on the left with the flag flying in front is Brant's house. On the far right is Mohawk Chapel.

and his ability to redistribute his wealth — good qualities in any leader.

The Mohawks collectively preserved ties with friends and allies in other parts of the colony. The war had destroyed the multicultural Mohawk Valley communities but simultaneously had created new ones through military service. Each year, at the beginning of May, the Mohawk Village hosted a reunion of Loyalists who had served in the Indian Department, Brant's Volunteers, or Butler's Rangers. Many veterans had received land grants a hundred kilometres away along the south shore of Lake Ontario and the west bank of the Niagara River, and the

Mohawks did not want distance to erode friendships. Families travelled from across the Niagara peninsula to visit old neighbours, to reminisce about life before the war and to recount the harrowing events of their wartime service. Alcohol, dancing, and horse racing contributed to the festivities and to a shared sense of community.

Canajoharies also tried to recreate the human geography of the Mohawk Valley at the Grand River by inviting many non-Native Mohawk Valley families and former members of Brant's Volunteers to settle there. A few of these families appear to have been among the earliest settlers on the Grand. They included Hendrick Nelles and his two sons, Adam Young and his three sons, John Dochsteder, and Hendrick and John Huff. The Nelleses, Youngs, and Dochsteder all hailed from the Mohawk Valley and had served either in the Indian Department or in Butler's Rangers during the war. The Huffs fought with Brant in the Volunteers. Although doubtless the invitation to settle came from Brant, in February 1787, a council of Mohawks, Oneidas, Onondagas, Cayugas, and Delawares confirmed the Loyalists in their lands with the stipulation that the lands never be sold. The grants were extensive, extending three miles back of the river.

Only a favoured few received such large grants. Many Loyalists leased land. The Canajoharies had leased land to Palatines in the decades before the Revolution, and those tenants had staunchly defended the Mohawks during their troubles with George Klock, a fact that may have persuaded the Canajoharies to re-establish the practice at the Grand River. Over a period of years, Brant rented lots as large as twelve hundred acres, but more commonly between one hundred and four hundred acres, to friends, political allies, and former Loyalist soldiers. In some cases, the rents were purely symbolic, with some families delivering one pepper-corn per year for 999 years. Other contracts carried substantial rents in cash or in produce to raise an income for the Haudenosaunee. Given the miserly price the British government paid for Aboriginal lands, Brant's leases earned more money for the Six Nations than land sales ever would.

Leases and grants created a variety of settlement patterns. Some Loyalists congregated in clusters, the largest being the Nelles settlement, which would contain about thirty families in 1828. Other Loyalists lived interspersed with the Aboriginal inhabitants of the river. Still others had married Haudenosaunee women and raised their children in their wives' community. The result was a complex, multicultural, multilingual community.

Brant was the most vocal proponent of limited grants and land leases, but many Onondagas, Cayugas, and Delawares supported his strategy. Still, several individuals and groups remained deeply sceptical of the plan. The harshest criticism of Brant's land policies came from

Tiononderoges, especially Isaac and Aaron Hill. Before the war, Tiononderoge had also fought to preserve its land against greedy colonists, but whereas the Canajoharies had enjoyed considerable local support in their struggle against Klock, Tiononderoge fought the anonymous Corporation of Albany alone. Seeing leases and grants as the thin end of the wedge leading to dispossession, the Hills threatened to kill Brant for "bringing white People to settle in their lands," and then decamped for the Bay of Quinte in 1788 or 1789. Opposition, however, remained confined. In 1796, thirty-five chiefs and headmen signed a power of attorney giving Brant the authority to sell even more of the land.

Throughout the ordeal of resettlement and the painful dispute with the Hills, Brant was missing a key ally. Molly Brant had not settled at Grand River. After a life of wandering, she and her children moved to the new town of Kingston (formerly Cataraqui), a small but bustling commercial and military centre at the east end of Lake Ontario. The family moved into a house built at government expense and lived on an annual pension of £100, the rewards of her "zealous Service" to the Crown. Nearby was another house for her brother, but it stood empty except when Joseph Brant was visiting Molly or passing through on his way to Montreal or Quebec. Molly Brant's decision not to reside at Grand River is curious, as she had devoted so much of her adult life to the public affairs of her people. Yet, she was a devoted and attentive mother, who had insisted her children receive an education wherever her duties took her. Brant likely believed that Kingston, however raw and unrefined, would afford her children more opportunities than Grand River. Indeed, all her children married well by Anglo-American standards. The eldest daughter, Elizabeth, married Robert Kerr an army surgeon and Indian Department doctor. Magdalene wed John Ferguson, who won election to the Assembly of Upper Canada. Two other daughters married army officers. While Brant's daughters moved in Anglo-American society, they did not renounce their mother's culture. Instead, through marriage they incorporated British men into

Elizabeth Kerr, the youngest child of Joseph and Catharine Brant, married William Johnson Kerr, Molly Brant and Sir William Johnson's grandson, in 1828. She died in 1844.

Haudenosaunee society, with the expectation that such unions would serve Haudenosaunee interests. Such alliances had served the Mohawks well in the past and promised to assist in the transition to Upper Canada.

Britain's failure to include its Native allies in the peace settlement forced First Nations to ratify separate treaties with an ebullient young republic that was in no mood to negotiate with "conquered" foes. By no means did Brant and other Aboriginal leaders consider themselves conquered,

but they also understood that the United States could dictate terms if they negotiated with each nation separately. Two prospects gave Brant hope, however. If First Peoples confederated, they could obtain a better treaty. The establishment of the United States also raised the possibility of reinstating the "playoff" system that had existed between Britain and France.

To achieve both those ends, Brant went west in August 1783 as a member of a large Six Nations delegation to speak with the people of the Ohio. At Sandusky, before a gathering of Delawares, Wyandots, Shawnees, Mingoes, and Ottawas, Brant delivered a speech advocating pan-Indianism. Reminding those present that all First Peoples shared the same interests, he urged unity in matters of peace and war. These ideas did not originate with Brant. The Ohio nations had been important members in the multi-national struggle that was Pontiac's War. The audience was receptive, but wary of Brant and the Mohawks' recent conversion to inter-tribal unity.

Despite Brant's exhortations, the Six Nations would be the first to negotiate a separate treaty with the United States. American leaders grasped the obstacles a confederacy would pose to western expansion and did everything in their power to divide and isolate nations. Congress, therefore, invited the Mohawks, Onondagas, Cayugas, and Senecas to a council at Fort Stanwix in the fall of 1784. The nations involved warily consented, but would send only a small delegation of war chiefs, with limited powers only to hear what the government had to say and then call for a general council. To confuse matters, New York State disputed Congress's authority to treat with the Six Nations and moved quickly to schedule a conference at Fort Stanwix before the federal agents could act. New York had originally intended to hold the meeting at the Mohawk Valley community of German Flats, but it was agreed to change venues because Brant's old neighbours and enemies "are generally unruly, and don't like to see Indians after the affair of General Herkermer."

Brant, sensing an opportunity to play the state against the federal government, accepted Governor Clinton's invitation on the condition Congressional representatives were also present. Upon arriving at Fort Stanwix, Clinton impatiently demanded the council begin, as the Congressional commissioners were nowhere in sight. New York aimed at nothing less than obtaining rights to all Six Nations' land within the state, and would brook no federal interference. Brant frustrated Clinton's plans at every turn. When Clinton demanded land as compensation for the destruction warriors had caused, Brant agreed to hand over only Niagara and Oswego. These were symbolic gestures, as the posts remained in British hands. When Clinton insisted on larger cessions, Brant replied that his party lacked authority to make further surrenders. Clinton could do no more, and left the council without adding any new territory to New York State.

Brant also left Fort Stanwix before the meeting with Congressional commissioners. Pressing matters, both public and private, demanded his immediate attention. Haldimand was retiring to England, and Brant wanted to obtain the deed for the Grand River lands before he left. Brant then hoped to travel with Haldimand to London, where he could advocate for Mohawk war claims in person and inquire whether Britain would assist the Six Nations should they become embroiled in another war with the United States. Before undertaking such an arduous journey, though, he went home to see his family. Catharine had given birth to a son, Joseph Jr., and Brant wanted to temporarily settle the family at their Kingston home until his return.

Brant reached Quebec before Haldimand's departure,

Fort Stanwix at the head of the Mohawk Valley hosted the 1784 treaty that ended the war between the Six Nations and the United States.

and much to his pleasure Haldimand issued a proclamation on October 25, 1784, conveying the Grand River tract to the Mohawks and Six Nations. On the surface, the document's wording seems unambiguous, permitting the

In London, Brant would have watched military displays such as the changing of the guard at St. James Park, depicted in an 1880 watercolour.

Mohawks "to take Possession of, & Settle upon the Banks of the River commonly called *Ours* [Ouse] or Grand River." However, the document did not stipulate on what terms the Mohawks would hold their lands, a conscious or unconscious oversight that would later become the source of much discord.

Meanwhile, a crisis had developed at Fort Stanwix. In Brant's absence, Aaron Hill was one of only two Mohawk delegates to meet with federal representatives. The commissioners, Oliver Wolcott, Arthur Lee, and Richard Butler, announced the Six Nations were not "a free and independent nation" but a "subdued people" and dictated terms under threat of force. The commissioners took

hostages, including Hill, to ensure the return of approximately one hundred captives still living in Haudenosaunee villages. The subsequent treaty ceded to the federal government all Seneca lands west of a boundary line drawn four miles east of the Niagara River from Lake Ontario to Buffalo Creek.

News of Hill's imprisonment reached Brant in Quebec, forcing him to postpone his trip to England and return to Grand River. By the time he arrived, others had already arranged for Hill's release. Brant spent much of the next year attending to business at Grand River and Niagara and taking time out to participate in a council in which the Six Nations renounced the Treaty of Fort Stanwix as a gross fraud. Not until November 1785 did Brant set sail for England, and then against John Johnson's wishes. Johnson feared Brant's questions concerning whether Britain would support First Peoples militarily would embarrass the government.

Brant found London swarming with Loyalists and Indian Department officers seeking favours, appointments, and half pay. Among those he encountered lingering around government offices were his colleagues Daniel Claus, Guy Johnson, and John Butler. As a group, they visited the secretary of state, Lord Sydney, of whom Joseph pointedly asked whether the Six Nations could expect assistance should another war break out. Sydney deferred responding for nearly three months, giving Brant plenty of time to reacquaint himself with the city and its people. To entertain himself, Brant accompanied Daniel Claus and his son William to a freak show and later attended masquerade balls. He dined with the Prince of Wales and again received an audience with King George III. He also sat for two portraits, one by John Francis Rigaud, which was later destroyed by fire, and another by American artist Gilbert Stuart. With Claus, Brant finally completed the *Mohawk Prayer Book* he had begun years earlier with John Stuart. Claus had the book published the following year.

As Brant prepared to board ship for the return voyage in April, he could only conclude the London trip had been only partially successful. The government was eager to

Joseph Brant sat for this portrait by Gilbert Stuart during his trip to London in the winter of 1785-86.

reward the Mohawks for their past services, but balked at making any commitments for the future. While Brant had received a government pension, compensation for himself and Molly, and about £15,000 for the Mohawks' losses —

much richer payments than the Loyalists had received — Sydney had given him no reason to believe Britain would risk another war with the United States on behalf of its Native allies. Disappointed, Brant sailed for Canada, for there was nothing left for him to do in England.

Government officials who spoke with Brant on his return noted a shocking change in his personality. After a long voyage, during which he had ample opportunity to brood on his grievances, Brant had frankly, if imprudently, criticized the government and its ministers. He ridiculed Sydney for being a "stupid Blockhead," causing some old friends to begin questioning his loyalty. Yet, the loyalty they spoke of was a distinctly European quality, inextricably bound up in the ranked orders of Europe and expressed as fealty to the king. Deference and obedience had no place among First Peoples, who lived in a world structured by relatively egalitarian kinship relationships. The Haudenosaunee considered themselves as equals to the king and well within their rights to criticize his or his minister's behaviour.

Brant, too, noticed changes in the way officials behaved towards him, as wary British officers treated him with greater care and circumspection. The relationship between Brant and John Johnson, which had never been warm, strained visibly. Johnson distrusted Brant's ambitions, blamed him for the dispute with the Hills, and opposed his land policies generally. Constant rumours of war, either with the Americans or with First Nations, further weakened relations between Brant and the British. One day in 1789, as Brant entered Fort Niagara, a sentry demanded he surrender his arms. A proud warrior, he bristled at the idea of surrendering the symbols of his position and status. The commandant intervened and allowed Brant to keep his weapons, but the incident underscored how much the relationship had deteriorated.

To remind the British of his diplomatic value, Brant attended councils in the United States and flirted with American officials. The United States wanted Brant to help avert a crisis in the west. Following the 1784 Treaty of Fort Stanwix, United States commissioners signed a similarly harsh treaty with the Wyandots, Delawares, Chippawas, and Ottawas at Fort McIntosh in the Ohio Valley on January 21, 1785. Militants denounced the treaty and, with British supplies, began to raid American settlements. In October 1791, General Josiah Harmar led a punitive expedition into the Ohio. Although American soldiers burned several villages, warriors inflicted more than a hundred casualties on Harmar's army, forcing the Americans to retreat.

Etching of view of London Bridge

Faced with armed resistance and an empty treasury, Secretary of War Henry Knox moved towards a more conciliatory policy that recognized the First Peoples' right to occupy their lands. Even so, he continued to assert that the United States held the underlying title to the soil. Moreover, efforts to keep the Six Nations out of the Ohio conflict induced the United States to negotiate a new, more balanced relationship with the Six Nations.

In the competition for loyalties, neither the United

States nor Britain could take the Six Nations for granted. Both powers actively courted prominent chiefs and headmen with expensive presents, and in so doing revived the playoff system. Federal and New York State officials, believing that Brant had more influence with the Ohio nations than he really had, worked hard to bring Brant into their particular camp. Brant corresponded extensively with Knox, Clinton, and federal Indian Commissioner Timothy Pickering, raising more red flags about his loyalty to Britain. Brant was no mercenary selling his services to the highest bidder. Rather, he played on the fears of both the United States and Great Britain in order to moderate each power's Indian policies. He wanted the United States to negotiate a peace deal with the western confederacy as a whole, rather than with individual nations. And he wanted the British to know he was talking with American officials, for it would help him obtain British assistance in the defence of First Peoples' lands.

Yet, from his trip to London, Brant knew that the British would refuse to assist the western nations in the event of full-blown war with the United States. Therefore, he urged the confederacy to achieve peace on favourable terms. Resistance might be necessary, but only if it led to a negotiated settlement with the United States. In trying to both organize and moderate the western nations, Brant faced numerous obstacles. For one, he could not overcome history. In 1737, the Six Nations Confederacy had sold Delaware lands from beneath their feet at the infamous Walking Purchase. Then again, in 1768, they had sold Shawnee, Delaware, and Mingo lands in the Ohio Valley. The westerners reasonably doubted the professed good intentions of the Six Nations, and Brant's moderation made him seem like an Anglo-American tool. In June 1791, militants challenged Brant to take up the hatchet

Large wampum belts signified important treaties and other agreements. Note the figures on the belt are holding hands, or linking arms, a common Haudenosaunee metaphor for alliance and unity.

against the Americans. Refusing, Brant surrendered any pretensions to leadership of the confederacy.

In the west, the task of crushing the confederacy fell to the governor of the Northwest Territory, Arthur St. Clair, and an army of fourteen hundred mostly raw recruits. On November 4, 1791, a combined force of Miamis, Shawnees, Delawares, Potawatomis, Ottawas, Chippewas, Wyandots, Mingoes, and Cherokees defeated and routed St. Clair's army. Conspicuous by their absence, the Six Nations further alienated themselves from the western nations. Victorious warriors taunted Brant by sending him the bloody scalp of Richard Butler, one of the federal commissioners responsible for the Treaty of Fort Stanwix, and a message asking, "You chief Mohawk, what are you doing? Time was when you roused us to war, & told us that if all the Indians would join with the King they should be a happy people & become independent. In a very short time you changed your voice & went to sleep & left us in the lurch."

Above: General Wayne constructed Fort Defiance in August 1794 at the confluence of the Glaize and Maumee Rivers as a base of operations for the final campaign against the western confederacy.
Below: The calumet or peace pipe smoked by the signers of the Treaty of Greeneville to show their agreement.

back into the United States. Brant declined but believed the United States was willing to negotiate a boundary with the Ohio nations. While Washington pursued a negotiated settlement, General "Mad Anthony" Wayne had replaced the hapless St. Clair and was relentlessly training a new army near Pittsburgh.

At a council in the summer of 1793, Brant and other moderate leaders counselled their allies to make the most of recent military successes and negotiate a compromise boundary line that recognized American settlements north of the Ohio River. The militants, encouraged by Alexander McKee, an Indian Department officer, rejected Brant's proposal and insisted that the Ohio River should become the dividing line between them and the United States.

Despite these reverses, American leaders continued to have an exaggerated impression of Brant's influence and hoped to use the Mohawk leader to keep the Six Nations from assisting the western confederacy. Accordingly, Knox invited Brant to Philadelphia in May 1792. Brant must have felt as if he were back in London the way President Washington and his cabinet feted him and offered various bribes and inducements to lure the Mohawks

While these negotiations took place, Wayne had completed preparations to invade the Ohio. After constructing Fort Defiance on the Glaize River, Wayne advanced towards the British-held Fort Miamis. On August 20, 1794, warriors attacked the American army on a

American cavalry flanked and routed warriors at the Battle of Fallen Timbers. Charge of the Dragoons at Fallen Timbers, *painted by R. T. Zogbaum, ca. 1895, illustrates General Anthony Wayne's campaign in 1794.*

patch of ground called Fallen Timbers, so called because a tornado had toppled all of the trees in the area. As Wayne's soldiers drove the warriors towards the nearby fort, the British garrison closed the gates, leaving the warriors to their fate. The western confederacy collapsed.

Later that year, Britain again enraged its First Nations allies. In November, John Jay negotiated a treaty with the British that bears his name. Amongst other things, the Jay Treaty required Britain to abandon posts within the boundaries of the United States. Together the destruction of the western confederacy and the establishment of firm bound-aries between British North America and the United States spelled the end of the short-lived playoff system.

Brant successfully made the transition from war to peace, from warrior to diplomat. This was not new. Warriors had engaged in Haudenosaunee politics at least since early con-tact with Europeans and probably earlier. What was new was the unprecedented degree to which warriors like Brant came to dominate their people's councils after 1783. Indeed, Brant transcended traditional clan and village

After Fallen Timbers, the United States dictated terms members of the western confederacy at the Treaty of Greeneville in 1795.

affiliations and spoke for a large, multi-ethnic constituency. It is possible to exaggerate Brant's power as a spokesperson for the Grand River. Indeed, Anglo-Americans often mistook orators who spoke for chiefs and headmen for the people they represented. The frequency with which critics, the Hills for example, identified certain policies with Brant, however, suggests that Brant was no empty vessel. Rather, he had transformed his wartime alliances into a broad-based peacetime coalition capable of forwarding a specific agenda.

Yet, by the end of 1794, much of what Brant had worked towards since the end of the Revolution had come unravelled. Beyond obtaining compensation for himself and his people, he had been unable to persuade Britain to uphold its alliance commitments to the Haudenosaunee. The western confederacy that he had helped to create and which he aspired to lead had rejected his leadership and then had been defeated. Only the settlement of the Grand River had succeeded. Thwarted abroad, Brant would increasingly attend to the business and welfare of the Grand River.

CHAPTER 5
ISOLATION

I n the early spring of 1795, Joseph Brant's public and private lives, never far apart, collapsed in on each other. His eldest son, Isaac, shot and killed a man near his home at Grand River. The victim, a man named Lowell, a deserter from Anthony Wayne's army, had come to the Grand to ply his trade as a saddle- and harness-maker. The reckless killing was the latest in a string of violent incidents involving Isaac. Earlier he had incited a riot in Detroit. The murder stunned the community and sent shockwaves through the colony. That Isaac had without provocation coolly pulled the trigger in front of witnesses was only one reason the incident received widespread attention and commentary. Lowell's murder channelled political tensions that had been building between Joseph Brant and the colonial administration for more than two years and now threatened to burst into open conflict.

The underlying strain between Brant and the colony's lieutenant-governor, John Graves Simcoe, centred on land. Brant, who had already leased and granted land to a number of Loyalists, proposed selling more land and investing the proceeds to create an income for the Six Nations. His goal was to improve the quality of life for his people and to make the Grand River economically self-sustaining and

Many Onondagas supported Brant's policy of limited grants and land leases. This painting depicts Thouhama, or Sweet Grass, an Onondaga chief's wife, at Grand River, at a slightly later period, early nineteenth century.

Burlington Bay, also known as the Head of the Lake, in June 1796. Here two years later Brant began building his mansion.

politically independent of Great Britain. Simcoe quashed the plan by resolutely denying that the Haudenosaunee had the legal right to sell lands to anyone but the Crown.

Focusing exclusively on land, however, obscures the larger issue at stake: Haudenosaunee sovereignty. Independence originated with the possession of productive land, and no people with pretensions to sovereignty could surrender control of this most basic resource. If the Haudenosaunee were a free and independent people, as they had maintained all along, then they had to be able to sell their land to whomever they chose.

Lowell's murder forced Brant and Simcoe to confront these issues head on. As the murder took place at Grand River, and involved two residents, the Mohawks viewed the incident as an internal matter to be resolved according to their own customs. However, because the victim was a "white" man, the government insisted on adjudicating the case before a judge in a courtroom. Officials could admit neither that Lowell had become a member of a predominantly Haudenosaunee community nor that the Six Nations possessed the authority to mete out justice. Brant rejected the very assumptions on which the administration came to these conclusions. Doubtless, he wanted to protect his son from the punitive English legal system, but he also had to fend off colonial officials who sought to extend the state's legal authority over the Grand River. To permit a trial in the colonial courts would be an admission that the Six Nations possessed only limited sovereignty.

Simcoe, however, was prepared to risk a confrontation by removing Isaac from Grand River by force. Guy Carleton, who had returned to Quebec in 1786 with the title Baron Dorchester and the appointment of governor-in-chief, refused to grant Simcoe permission. Dorchester believed that the death of an American deserter was hardly

Isolation

worth a showdown with Brant. When informed of Simcoe's intent, Brant reportedly bragged, "it would be seen who had [the] most Interest with the Militia, and that the Governor would not be able to make them Act against him." The boast may have been gratuitous, but it was well known that many of the settlers at Grand River owed their land and livelihoods to the Six Nations and were personal friends of Brant. In 1798, a Moravian missionary passing through the tract noted that "all the settlers are in a kind of vassalage to him [Brant]." It was for just this reason that Simcoe had adamantly opposed the Six Nations selling or leasing land to settlers. He feared that a

The Indian Department distributed presents annually to the Six Nations at the Head of the Lake.

conjunction of Native and non-Native residents would undermine loyalty to the Crown and permit competing sovereignties within the colony. The colonial strategy of divide and rule ran square up against Haudenosaunee attempts to incorporate individuals through adoption and the construction of alliances among groups of people.

Isaac unwittingly resolved the crisis later that year. During the annual distribution of presents at the Head of the Lake (present-day Burlington), Isaac drank too much in one of the taverns and loudly denounced his father, who happened to be in the next room. Joseph commanded Isaac to be silent. Father and son quarrelled until Isaac stabbed at Joseph with a knife. Joseph deflected the blow with his hand and struck Isaac on the head with a dagger. Friends removed the wounded Isaac to Grand River, where he died. Isaac's death would haunt Joseph Brant for the rest of his life.

Perhaps as early as 1790, Brant had begun formulating an idea that would eventually mature into the plan to sell the lands north of the Mohawk Village to create an annuity for

the Six Nations. The Grand River contained more acreage than the Haudenosaunee could cultivate, but was too small to allow men to earn their living from the hunt, a problem that would grow worse as expanding settlements destroyed game habitats. One obstacle blocking the sales was the fact that the Six Nations did not hold the deed to the lands and, therefore, could not transfer legal title to potential purchasers. Haldimand's proclamation was insufficient for this purpose, and no one would buy the land without secure title. Simcoe's response to Brant's request for a deed embroiled the two men in a prolonged public dispute and engendered lasting personal enmities.

Simcoe had arrived in Upper Canada in June 1792, the first lieutenant-governor of a colony that had been summoned into being a year earlier by the Constitutional Act of 1791. The deeply conservative Simcoe positively brimmed with energy and enthusiasm. He shared with his superiors the belief that an excess of democracy had caused the American Revolution, and he sought to correct this defect by creating an ordered and hierarchical society in Upper Canada. Inculcating British constitutional, political, and legal principles in the residents would keep democratic

John Graves Simcoe in 1791, the year he became Upper Canada's first lieutenant-governor.

followed an earlier survey that located the northern limit of the tract not at the river's source, as Haldimand had promised, but considerably short of that point. The missing block would be a source of conflict to the present day. Second, the Patent specifically and unambiguously denied the Haudenosaunee the right to sell, lease, or grant any portion of their land to private individuals. Only the government could legally purchase land from the First Peoples.

In offering the Six Nations less than they desired or expected, Simcoe had conformed to the conditions of the Royal Proclamation of 1763, which prohibited private purchases of Native lands. Simcoe and other imperial officials interpreted the proclamation to mean the First Nations did not own the land they inhabited, but possessed only the right of occupancy, while underlying title belonged to the Crown. Initially, Haudenosaunee may have neglected the document's expressly colonial undertones, as the upper nations of the Confederacy had no desire to sell their lands and its restrictions had had no effect on the Mohawks who lived east of the line.

Brant rejected the Simcoe Patent. While Simcoe and other British officials had couched their refusals to acknowledge Haudenosaunee ownership of the land in paternalistic language — Indians had to be saved from themselves — Brant understood that Simcoe's paternalism struck at Haudenosaunee sovereignty and could not be accepted without also admitting dependence on Great Britain.

John Baptiste Rousseaux's powder horn

tendencies in check. That his plans were completely detached from the realities of life in the rude and thinly settled province does not seem to have occurred to the ebullient Simcoe. Yet, his determination to restore and enhance royal authority over the colony's inhabitants bode ill for the Six Nations, whom he saw as dependents of the Crown.

The "patent" Simcoe offered Brant on January 14, 1793, reflected his understanding of the imperial hierarchy. The patent reaffirmed the Haldimand Proclamation, but with two important exceptions. First, the document

Simcoe had also intended the patent's blanket rejection of land grants and leases to serve as a warning to Brant and the Loyalists who held Grand River lands that he considered their arrangements illegal. Ejecting all of the settlers from the Grand River would have been no easy matter. The large numbers involved made removal a practical impossibility. Many Loyalists and Indian Department officers had

Beasley Hollow, Hamilton, Ontario, painted by John Herbert Caddy around 1860. This location was named for Brant's friend Richard Beasley who, together with James Wilson and Jean Baptiste Rousseaux, purchased Block 2.

married Haudenosaunee women before, during, or after the war, and had become thoroughly integrated into their wives' communities. John Dochsteder lived near the mouth of the Grand River with his second wife, an Onondaga woman. His first wife, a Cayuga, had died. It was in part to provide for his two daughters that the Haudenosaunee had granted Dochsteder a large tract of land fronting the river. Further up the river Loyalist John Young and his Mohawk wife lived on a tract of land given to him in council by chiefs and headmen. Although such unions doubtlessly reflected a calculated strategy to incorporate important Euro-Americans into Haudenosaunee society, they also produced stable and loving families that blurred and complicated tidy racial categories. To remove these men or take away their lands would break up long-established families and divide the community. Simcoe did

not move against the multicultural communities of the Grand River, but he threatened to, all the while holding the Royal Proclamation over their heads.

There the matter lay for some time. Without the deed, Brant did not pursue the land sales. Finally, in the early months of 1795, Brant took advantage of Simcoe's temporary absence from the capital at Niagara to negotiate the first of several major land deals. In March, Philip Stedman, who operated the Niagara portage, purchased twelve square miles of land that would become known as Block 1. Later Brant sold a similar-sized tract, Block 2, to Richard Beasley, a miller and trader living at the Head of the Lake, and his two associates James Wilson and Jean Baptiste Rousseaux, Brant's son-in-law. By the end of 1796, he had sold four large blocks, alienating the northern half of the Grand River tract. Two more blocks sold the following year. Providing everyone paid the agreed-upon price, the Six Nations anticipated receiving more than £85,000. The interest on that sum would net about £5,119 annually. No First Nations had ever received such a high price for their lands. To legitimate and facilitate the land transactions, Grand River chiefs granted Brant a power of attorney in November. Still, in order to secure the purchasers in their lands, deeds were required.

Returning from his sojourn to eastern Upper Canada, Simcoe now faced the uncomfortable fact that Brant had sold lands in defiance of the royal will. He disallowed the land sales, but did nothing more. Tired, ill, and disillusioned with Upper Canada, Simcoe requested and received permission to leave the province. He departed in July and would never return.

Brant, too, left Upper Canada in early 1797 in order to press his claim for a deed to the Grand River lands. Originally, he had planned to go to England, but the poor state of his finances would not permit such a costly venture. Instead, he decided to go to Philadelphia, the American capital, to visit the British minister, Robert Liston. The capital city (Washington did not become the capital till 1800) would provide fertile ground for the seeds of doubt and fear he intended to sow.

Arriving at Philadelphia in February, Brant vented his spleen about his treatment at the hands of British authorities. Word of Brant's dissatisfaction reached Liston even before the two men had met. What alarmed the minister most were rumours that, if Brant did not obtain satisfaction, he would join a French army that was expected (incorrectly) to invade Upper Canada. Doubtless, Brant intended the bluster to frighten Liston into settling on the Mohawk's terms. Brant further preyed on Liston's fears by associating exclusively with Republicans, the pro-French party of opposition, to the extent that he snubbed outgoing president George Washington and his Anglophile Federalist Party. Brant's flirtations with the Republicans alarmed British officials and compounded fears of a

French invasion. With the Six Nations occupying the colony's exposed western flank, officials were right to worry about the identity of Brant's dinner companions.

In March, on his return home, Brant stopped in Albany, where he met with John Deserontyon of the Quinte Mohawks and New York's Indian commissioners. Together, Brant and Deserontyon agreed to sell their remaining lands in the Mohawk Valley for $1,000 and collected $600 to cover their travelling expenses. Stopping next at Canandaigua, New York, Brant complained of being slighted by federal officials in Philadelphia. Washington should have complained of Brant's behaviour, but government officials nonetheless ordered that Brant be paid $400 to correct the perceived offence.

Returning to the Grand River, Brant found conditions ripe to push his advantage. Simcoe's temporary replacement, Peter Russell, was no more inclined than Simcoe to allow the sales to proceed, but, unlike Simcoe, Russell did not have the stomach for a prolonged confrontation. War with France seemed imminent, and a tragic event in 1796 highlighted the province's vulnerability. In August of the previous year, the Mississauga chief Wabakinine and his family had camped outside the new capital at York (Toronto). One night, a British soldier named Charles McCuen came into Wabakinine's camp in order to sleep with the chief's sister. Apparently, the two had prearranged the encounter without her brother's knowledge. When Wabakinine awoke after a night of drinking, he saw an intruder in the camp and lunged forward to protect his sister. McCuen smashed the chief's head with a rock, inflicting a wound that would prove fatal. Although he was arrested on murder charges, a jury acquitted McCuen for lack of evidence, an all-too-common outcome in cases involving Aboriginal people. The death of Wabakinine, a signatory to several land cessions, including the Grand River surrender, and the acquittal of the murderer incensed the Mississaugas. When a hasty distribution of presents and rum did not appease the growing crowd of Mississaugas, the administration began to fear that the chiefs were planning

A Mississauga hunter and his wife in Upper Canada, painted by Charles Dawson Shanly in the period 1837-1847.

York as it looked in 1796, when Brant made his trip there to petition Russell to sell Grand River lands.

to revolt. Many wondered what part Brant would play.

No rebellion materialized. Some scholars have credited Brant with diffusing the tense situation. Whatever the Mohawk's role in scotching an armed revolt, Brant did seek closer ties with Wabakinine's people and invited the Mississaugas to the Mohawk Village's annual May festival. There the Mississaugas appointed Brant to replace Wabakinine and entrusted him with the management of their lands. The Haudenosaunee and Mississaugas had long been enemies — the Haudenosaunee derided the Mississaugas for stinking like fish, a reference to the fish oil the latter applied to their bodies — but historic enmities succumbed to the necessity of presenting a united front to the British. Brant and the Mississauga chiefs would work together. As a sign of solidarity, Mississauga warriors shaved their heads into scalp locks in imitation of the Mohawks.

Alarmed at the conjunction of Aboriginal groups, Russell instructed Indian Department officers to "foment any existing Jealousy between the Chippewas [Mississaugas] & the Six Nations; and to prevent ... any Junction or good understanding between those two Tribes." In June 1797, Lieutenant James Givins received an appointment to act as agent to the Mississaugas with orders to keep the Mississauga and Six Nations apart. The government sought to prevent fraternization by delivering presents to the two groups at different times and places rather than at one central location. Disgusted at the new turn in Indian affairs, Brant warned that such innovations "might tend to bad consequences by disuniting us, and depriving us of the liberty of enjoying our old Customs."

At the same time he was fashioning a new pan-Indian alliance, Brant hammered away at Russell to confirm the Grand River sales. "The present critical situation of public affairs," Russell wrote, "obliges me to refrain from taking that notice of Capt. Brant's conduct on this occasion which it deserves." Knowing that acceding to the Mohawk's demands would be seen as capitulation by his superiors in faraway London, Russell dissembled and delayed until he received some orders. In June, Brant appeared in York demanding that the land sales proceed. A besieged Russell asked for the particulars in writing, which he promised to present to the Executive Council. The reply left Russell thunderstruck. Rather than deny the Mohawk's demands, as Russell had predicted, Council members, fearing the Six Nations would support the predicted French invasion, urged the government to comply with all of Brant's demands.

In July, before Russell could finalize the land sales, the long-awaited instructions arrived from England. Home secretary the Duke of Portland had expressly prohibited the land sales. With orders in hand, Russell returned to the Executive Council and asked whether, in light of Portland's orders, he should break his promise to Brant, to which the Council unanimously voted "No." Councilmen argued that the safety of the province superseded orders. Russell should convey the lands to the Six Nations without restriction.

Ignoring Council's advice, Russell informed Brant that Portland had forbidden the land sales, but the government was willing to grant the Six Nations an annuity equal to what they expected to raise from the sales. Unwilling to accept any settlement that left the Haudenosaunee so obviously dependent on government, Brant turned to leave. Knowing that Brant "had great Influence not only with his own Tribe, but with the rest of the five Nations, and most of the neighboring Indians; and that he was very capable of doing much mischief," Russell hastily recalled the Mohawk. The two men struck a deal that allowed the land

A view of the new Loyalist settlement of Queenston, a few miles south of Niagara, from the American side of the Niagara River.

sales to proceed on the condition that the Six Nations would surrender the lands to the Crown, which in turn would convey the assigned tracts to the purchasers. In this way, Russell kept within the bounds of the Royal Proclamation. A few days later, the agreement was confirmed at a public council meeting.

After the necessary paperwork was completed, the sales took place on February 5, 1798. Brant officially transferred the lands to Russell who, in the king's name, conveyed the blocks to their several purchasers. Over 380,000 acres had passed from the Six Nations to speculators. As the Six Nations were not subjects of the Crown, they required three non-Native trustees to manage the monies raised by the land sales. Brant selected Alexander Stewart, a Niagara lawyer and the husband of a Mohawk woman, D.W. Smith, a legislator and friend of Brant's, and William Claus, Daniel Claus's son.

Many historians have interpreted the showdown between Brant and Russell as a victory for the former, yet it was Brant not Russell who had conceded the most. Russell had forced Brant to comply with British demands requiring First Nations to sell land only to the Crown. Brant had earlier rejected Simcoe's patent for that very reason. But by 1797, Brant had little choice. No one would purchase land

The British built Fort George on the Upper Canadian side of the Niagara River after the Jay Treaty forced them to abandon Fort Niagara in 1796. The fort became the site for many important councils with the Six Nations.

when the title was in dispute, and if the sales did not go through, there could be no annuity. Moreover, the protracted struggle over the legality of First Peoples' land sales and leases had made many Grand River leaseholders nervous, and some Loyalist families had abandoned their farms. Had Brant refused Russell's terms, he would have further jeopardized the lands of his friends and allies.

In September, another dispatch arrived from London that dispirited Brant and Russell equally. The imperial government had reassigned responsibility for Indian affairs in Upper Canada from the military, represented by John Johnson, to the lieutenant-governor of the province. Russell was appalled that he now bore primary responsibility for dealing with people he did not understand or like.

Brant saw the reform for what it was, an attempt to drive wedges between First Peoples and the Indian Department. These reforms were the first major structural reorganization of the Department since William Johnson had been appointed superintendent in 1755.

Although John Johnson remained the titular head of Indian affairs, Russell held the real power. That, combined with John Butler's death in 1796 and the appointment of men such as James Givins, effectively isolated Brant and the Six Nations from the upper echelons of the department. Before leaving Indian affairs to civil authorities, Johnson did manage to have his nephew William Claus appointed to replace Butler. If Brant expected Claus to continue in the tradition of William Johnson and John

Joseph Brant's mansion at the Head of the Lake, Ontario, 1804.

Butler, he was mistaken. The young man adopted the smothering paternalism of his superiors. In particular, he denied that the First Peoples had the right to sell their land, putting him at odds with Brant. When the two men clashed, Claus used the powers of his office to cultivate anti-Brant factions at Grand River.

Despite these setbacks, the sale of the blocks did produce a small income for the Six Nations, although not as much or as regularly as anyone would have liked. With the annuity, Brant lessened the Grand River's dependence on the British government. In time, the Six Nations assumed the responsibility for paying the community's blacksmith, doctor, schoolteacher, surveyor, and lawyer. They also built a new council house and mill with proceeds from the sales.

Nevertheless, even though land sales did allow the Six Nations a greater degree of independence, proceeds fell far short of expectations and generated domestic opposition to Brant and his policies.

In 1798, Brant began building a new house near Burlington Bay. Although he and Catharine would not move until 1802 or 1803, the project indicated his intention to eventually move away from the Grand River. The hard-fought battles over land had scarred Brant at home, where his policies came under increasing criticism. Less than three months after Russell had approved the sales, several of the purchasers had fallen behind in their

The exterior of Joseph Brant Museum in Burlington, Ontario, a reconstruction of Brant's original house.

been stripped of his deed, and another had died in debtors' prison. Only Brant's old friend, the wealthy merchant Richard Beasley, made regular payments, and even he wanted to surrender some of his land and renegotiate the mortgage.

By 1801, Brant was being pressed from two sides: a growing domestic opposition and the government. During a council that year, a group consisting principally of Tiononderoge Mohawks — people Brant derided as a few "Lower [Tiononderoge] Mohawks without a chief" — forced him to promise to retire by the spring. In his stead, twenty-four chiefs were appointed to oversee land matters. Brant outmanoeuvred his enemies on this occasion, as the chiefs insisted that Brant stay on as the agent responsible for land matters. The next year, Lieutenant-Governor Hunter issued a proclamation prohibiting First Peoples from leasing their lands. The proclamation applied to past as well as future leases. All of the Grand River Loyalists could be removed and the community Brant had created would be dissolved.

At the same time, the block sales had engendered bitter recrimination. Brant and the trustees, with the exception of D.W. Smith, grew to dislike each other intensely and communicated little. William Claus, who was more intent on discrediting Brant than in serving Haudenosaunee interests, interfered and meddled in the land transactions to the detriment of the Six Nations. While government officers wanted to confiscate the lands of all the delinquents, Brant insisted that Beasley, Wilson, and Rousseaux, who had made honest efforts to pay their debts, retain the lands they had paid for.

payments, and Brant asked the trustees to transfer the deed from one of the delinquents to another buyer. These failures undermined Brant's authority. Tiononderoge Mohawks and young warriors especially denounced both the policies that had led to land sales and Brant himself.

Despite domestic opposition, however, Brant continued to press Russell and his successor, Lieutenant-Governor Peter Hunter, for clear title to the rest of the Grand River and to allow further land sales. Armed with clear instructions from London, both men refused to yield. Brant then turned his attention to the other side of the border and proposed purchasing land south of Lake Erie that could be sold for a profit. To American officials, Brant explained that he had become so dissatisfied with the British that he wanted to remove with some of his people to the United States.

While Brant negotiated for lands in the United States (the deal would never be finalized), the legal status of the blocks had become so confused as to defy correction. Five of six buyers had not made any payments. One had

Isolation

By 1806, Beasley's block had finally raised £9,000, but the other tracts showed no signs of producing any income for the Six Nations. No one knew which mortgagers had paid or how much. In one case, there was confusion over who actually owned one of the blocks.

Brant's dealings on behalf of the Mississaugas were no more successful. Peter Russell had been applying pressure on the Mississaugas to sell a valuable tract of land between the Head of the Lake and York. Brant demanded two shillings per acre — about half of what he received for Grand River lands, but a rate far higher than the two pence an acre paid for earlier cessions — and the right to reserve the valuable lands around the mouths of streams for the Mississaugas' use. Russell balked at the price and ordered the stoppage of presents to the Mississaugas. With game and fish stocks severely depleted, the Mississaugas could not long hold out against the government's coercive measures. Nor was Brant in any position to either assist them or to engage in a prolonged resistance. The Brant-Mississauga alliance soon collapsed. In 1802, the Mississaugas replaced Brant with another chief, and the flow of presents resumed. In 1805, chiefs finally agreed to sell 80,000 acres between York and the Head of the Lake for goods valued at £1,000.

In a final effort to have the Grand River lands confirmed to the Six Nations, Brant dispatched John Norton to England in 1804. In London, Norton met with singular success, winning over many of Brant's old friends and making allies of his own. On Hunter's orders, Claus immediately organized a council to repudiate Norton's

John Norton, as he appeared during his 1805 trip to England.

mission. The meeting was held at Buffalo Creek and attended primarily by New York Senecas. The chiefs would not recognize Norton's assignment and removed Brant from power. Had Brant been a chief, the senior women would have been responsible for deposing him. But Brant was not a chief, so it is unclear from what position he was being removed. Claus's stratagem was only partially successful, as the majority of chiefs and women at Grand River continued to support Brant. Nevertheless, Claus persuaded Buffalo Creek chiefs to repeat their performance at Fort George and had the proceedings sent to England. As part of the letter, Claus entirely misrepresented Norton as a "white" man playing at being an "Indian." Although Norton was half Cherokee and half Scot, he had been adopted by the Mohawks and accepted as one of their leaders. Claus's message and word of Brant's "overthrow" forced Norton to abandon his mission.

Brant responded during a July 1806 council at Fort George, where he ferociously denounced his opponents at Grand River and exposed Claus's duplicity in public council. He also requested that some other means be devised for transacting land business. The trustees, including Claus, no longer had the confidence of the Haudenosaunee. Claus, red with anger, stormed out of the meeting.

Receiving encouragement from the Duke of Northumberland, a member of the House of Lords who in 1776 had befriended the Mohawk while they were with Howe's army in New York, Brant again undertook a

The last portrait of Brant, by Ezra Ames, painted in 1806.

wearing his hair in a scalp lock. It was to be the last portrait of Brant. Brant returned home and continued to work tirelessly to make the blocks turn a profit, all the while pressing the government for a deed to the Grand River. With Brant and Claus at loggerheads, charges and counter-charges of fraudulent use of Six Nations' monies flew back and forth. Chronic financial problems and a disagreement over investment strategies even poisoned Brant's relationship with John Norton. Although the two men reconciled, the brief estrangement attests to the strains on Brant. In the fall of 1807, however, the financial situation began to improve, as Brant found a new purchaser for Block 5.

Before the negotiations were completed, Brant fell ill and took to his bed. In the past, Brant had suffered from painful attacks that temporarily incapacitated him. There was no reason this time to think that he would not recover. Neighbours came to sit and talk with the prostrate Brant. Some later recalled the topic was religion. Norton also came to visit, and it is reported that Brant told him, "Have pity on the poor Indians. If you can get any influence with the great, endeavour to do them all the good you can." Soon after, on November 24, 1807, Joseph Brant died. Isolated from the community he had struggled to create and defend, even with his last breath, Brant was buried at Burlington rather than at Grand River.

trip to England to settle land matters. This time, he made it only as far as Albany before running out of money. James Caldwell, Brant's Albany agent, opened his doors to the famous Mohawk and insisted that he sit for a portrait by a local artist named Ezra Ames. Ames's portrait reveals a heavy-set but healthy-looking sixty-four-year-old Brant,

EPILOGUE

Brant has bequeathed to subsequent generations a particularly complex and ambiguous legacy. He staunchly defended Haudenosaunee interests as he understood them, yet he appeared at times to promote assimilation. His support of Great Britain during the American Revolution contributed to the dispossession of the Mohawk people. After removing to Grand River, he spoke for the Six Nations, but his ideas and modes of thought were distinctly Canajoharie. His ambitious — some would say naive or corrupt — schemes to achieve the independence of Grand River led to greater dependence on the Crown. Seldom did Brant permit the confusion or self-doubt that he must have occasionally felt disturb the confidence he projected. Only at the height of the land dispute with Russell did he despair that "my sincere attachment [to England] has ruined the Interests of my Nation."

This 1859 painting of Blue Lake, Grand River, by Sir Daniel Wilson, captures the river much as it must have appeared in Brant's day.

No wonder Brant excites strong feelings among scholars and modern Haudenosaunee alike. Viewed from the vantage point of the present day, he appears to be a cultural chameleon, shifting effortlessly back and forth between Mohawk and English cultures. It is easy to be disappointed with him. Indeed, Brant could and did express different parts of his identity in different situations. He knew what words to speak and how to alter them depending upon his audience. In everyday life, he attended the Anglican Church, wore suits more often than breechcloths, and educated his children so they could read and write the English language better than he could. Secretly, perhaps, we would prefer that he acted more like Pontiac or Tecumseh, that he had led warriors in a brave but futile attempt to preserve his people's land and culture. Such desires say more about us than about Brant, more about the pervasive and pernicious idea that First Nations' cultures are static and unchanging, and more about an imagined past than about the hard realities and limited choices of living under colonialism.

Joseph Brant was a Mohawk. He embodied the broader changes Mohawks had found useful and necessary to live in a predominantly Anglo-American world. It says much about modern myopia when we fail to note that the Mohawks' German and Scots–Irish neighbours also found it useful and necessary to learn the Mohawk language and Haudenosaunee rituals. In important ways, the Mohawk and Grand River valleys were not racial frontiers but sites of cultural blending.

Nor should modern commentators fall into the ahistorical trap of judging Brant retrospectively. Knowing the outcome of Brant's transactions makes his strategies and

This Haudenosaunee headdress dates to 1900–1908 and follows a style typical of the Plains; it would not have been worn by warriors in the late eighteenth or early nineteenth centuries.

Epilogue

The Grand River in this pencil drawing by William Simpson, though it was rendered in 1855, looks much as it did in the 1790s and early 1800s when farms fronted the river.

methods appear like folly or worse. He seems to have been either naive to believe his schemes could have succeeded, or corrupt, lining his own pockets with the proceeds of land sales. Indeed, the record-keeping surrounding the block sales was atrocious, but much of the blame for the situation must be laid at the feet of the trustees, especially William Claus, who had responsibility for managing the investments. The pervasive paternalism of the day permitted government officials to treat Six Nations' money as their own. Such duplicitous dealings prevented the Six Nations from either reclaiming tracts that had not been paid for or salvaging something of value from their lands.

More concretely, Joseph Brant left both a powerful legacy and a burden to his family and his people. After his death, it fell to others to complete the work he had undertaken with such vigour and determination. Of course, he had

never acted alone. The support of chiefs and clan matrons had been critical to his endeavours, but, then as now, these policies were associated with him.

Catharine, like Margaret sixty years before, gathered her children and returned home after her husband's death. Life at the Head of the Lake had been luxurious but she had not been comfortable apart from other Canajoharies. Going back to the Mohawk Village, she would immerse her youngest children, John and Elizabeth, in Mohawk culture and link their destinies with those of their kinfolk. Together with her brother Tekarihogen, and John Norton, she would continue to pursue Brant's twin policies of having the Grand River lands confirmed to the Six Nations while pursuing land sales and leases as a means of raising income.

Of all Brant's children, John's life most closely followed that of his father's. Like Joseph, John received an education — in his case at the Mohawk Village, Ancaster, and Niagara — and became a warrior. At eighteen, he distinguished

Ruins of the Old naval Dept, at the mouth of the Grand River. Oct 1811

Construction of the naval depot at the mouth of the Grand River began after the War of 1812 but it was never completed and had fallen into ruin by 1840 when this painting was completed.

himself as a leader during the War of 1812. Together with John Norton, Tekarihogen, and his cousin William Johnson Kerr, Brant fought at Queenston Heights, Beaver Dams, Chippawa, and Lundy's Lane. These warriors did not command unanimous support. Perhaps the majority of Grand River Haudenosaunee preferred to remain neutral, while a significant minority had pro-American sympathies. These schisms reflected old divisions at Grand River. Those who opposed involvement in the war had also generally opposed Brant's land sales and leases. Their numbers had grown after Brant's death, because a number of squatters had taken up land at Grand River without the

Six Nations' permission. What motivated young, politically minded warriors to assist Britain in the War of 1812 was the opportunity to win prestige and to use military service to force concessions on the issue of Grand River lands from the Crown at a later date.

The war did advance John Brant's career, but colonial officials adamantly refused to recognize Haudenosaunee sovereignty over the Grand River lands. In 1821, meeting obstruction at home, Brant, together with another cousin, Robert Johnson Kerr, copied his father's tactics of going over the heads of colonial officials to appeal to their superiors in England. To all outward appearances, nothing had

Epilogue

A sketch of Brantford, Canada West, a decade after its founding in 1830.

changed in thirty years. London's luminaries feted the Mohawks. As the conversation turned to the Grand River lands, however, Brant found official opinion had shifted. Officials in the Colonial Office took a harder line and agreed to issue a deed only if the Six Nations relinquished claims to the disputed northern portion of the tract. After much negotiation, Brant and Kerr relented and accepted British terms. It was a partial victory to be sure, but it was more than his father had achieved.

Characteristically, the colonial government threw many obstacles in Brant's path. First, the administration, speaking through William Claus, argued that if the Haudenosaunee held their lands in fee simple, that is, like other settlers who had the right to buy and sell their land without encumbrance, then they would no longer be eligible to receive government presents. Despite this threat, a council of chiefs supported Brant. Shifting tactics, the

government then claimed that, by holding land in fee simple, the Six Nations implicitly acknowledged being subjects of the king. Consequently, they be would be subject to the laws of Upper Canada. This was too much for the chiefs, who backed out of the deal.

In 1828, Brant was appointed resident superintendent of the Six Nations of the Grand River, a position fraught with numerous difficulties and conflicts. The 1820s witnessed a sharp rise in the number of immigrants arriving in Upper Canada. Many families squatted on Haudenosaunee lands, exacerbating tensions and conflicts at Grand River. This new wave of settlers differed from those of Brant's day precisely because they took up land without permission or did so in agreement with individuals, not the council or the council's appointed representatives. As a result, the newcomers had no connections or personal ties to the Six Nations.

Captain John Brant, "Ahyouwaighs," who in 1830 received the chiefly title Tekarihogen from his mother, Catharine.

Another difficulty involved the ongoing rivalry between the Brant and Claus families. William Claus died of cancer of the lip in 1826, and his son John assumed his father's duties as trustee. Unfortunately, he also inherited his father's style of management. When Brant demanded the return of some lands granted to William before his death, John stopped paying the interest that had accrued on their investments. The dispute ended in 1830 when the government dismissed Claus.

One of the most pressing issues facing John Brant and the Six Nations involved the Welland Canal Company's proposal to build a dam across the Grand River to improve navigation. Opponents feared that rising water levels would destroy their homes and fields. Despite Brant's vigorous protests, construction proceeded and was completed in 1829. As predicted, the dam flooded large portions of the Grand River, sweeping away homes and farms.

John Brant more completely merged traditional and innovative forms of power than had his father. That was due, in part, to his mother, Catharine. After Tekarihogen died in 1830, it fell to Catharine to choose a successor. In consultation with the senior women of the turtle clan, she selected her son John to

Born in 1791, Catherine Brant John, the fifth and last surviving child of Joseph and Catharine Brant, died in 1867. She was buried at the Mohawk Chapel.

be the next Tekarihogen. As the leading Mohawk chief, a noted warrior, and an Indian agent, Brant held great promise for the future.

In the same year that he received his chiefly title, Brant also ran for a seat in the Legislative Assembly and won. Grand River settlers had elected a Mohawk, albeit one who lived more genteelly than most of his supporters, over John Warren, a veteran officer of the War of 1812, a magistrate, and a public servant. Perhaps Brant's relationship to Joseph Brant, from who many of the voters had obtained land, and his dogged defence of those lands against the Welland Canal Company propelled him to victory. Brant held the seat for less than a year, however, as the government ruled the leases held by most Grand River residents did not meet the

Catherine Elizabeth Kerr Osborne, granddaughter of Joseph Brant.

within two years of each other. John Norton had left Grand River in 1823 after killing a man in a duel. The man had had an affair with Norton's wife. Reportedly, he went to Mexico and never returned. Brant's enemies, too, were nearly all in the grave. His two great enemies, John Graves Simcoe and Peter Russell had died within a month of each other in the fall of 1808. William Claus passed away in 1826.

Pressure on Grand River lands continued to mount through the 1830s, as more settlers sought to make farms at the Six Nations' expense. The government's inability or unwillingness to stop the invasion of Haudenosaunee territory, persuaded many officials to consolidate the tract. In 1841, the Six Nations surrendered 220,000 acres to the Crown in exchange for a compact reserve of about 20,000 acres, exclusive of lands already being utilized along the river. Six years later, in 1847, the reserve was enlarged to about 50,000 acres. The money from the land sales paid for squatters' improvements and the remainder was invested — without the Six Nation's approval — in the Grand River Navigation Company. When the company went bankrupt in 1861, the Six Nations lost their entire investment. The reserve era transformed the Grand River into a more homogenous, Aboriginal community under the oversight of a paternalistic government.

In 1850, Mohawks exhumed Joseph Brant's body, which had lain at Burlington, and carried it in relays to Grand River, where he was re-interred at the Mohawk Chapel. After forty-three years, Brant returned to the community that had given him life and purpose. Community leaders may have orchestrated the return of Joseph Brant's

province's property-holding requirement for voters. The legislature overturned the election and gave the seat to Warren.

Both John Brant and John Warren perished in the cholera epidemic of 1832. Except for Catharine, who died exactly thirty years after her husband on November 24, 1837, most of the people associated with Joseph Brant were dead. John Johnson, Tekarihogen, and John Brant all died

Above: This painting of a railroad bridge over the Grand River, 1856, illustrates how human activities, such as land clearance, dams, and industrial development, have altered the region's landscape since Brant's day.
Below: Tin armbands typical of those worn by Mohawk warriors in Upper Canada.

body because the reserve, now surrounded by Anglo-American settlers, needed a touchstone with the past. Brant was someone who had both advocated engagement with Anglo-American society and resolutely defended Haudenosaunee interests. Such skills were desperately needed at the onset of the reservation period. Although he had been a contentious figure, he was now safely in the past and would not divide the community further.

Nearly four decades after the Mohawks had reclaimed Brant, the citizens of Brantford also staked a claim to the city's namesake. Founded in 1830, Brantford lay a little northwest of Mohawk Village on 807 acres ceded by the Six Nations. In 1886, the city erected a massive bronze-and-granite monument honouring the Mohawk.

Anglo-Canadian society has embraced Brant more completely and warmly than have the Haudenosaunee. Forgetting Brant's intense battles with colonial administrators, his ultimate desire to limit and control the people

These figures represent three of the Six Nations — from left to right, the Mohawk, Tuscarora, and Oneida — on the Joseph Brant Monument in Brantford, Ontario.

who settled at the Grand River, and his many flirtations with the United States, most Canadians misleadingly describe Brant as a Loyalist and subsume him within the smothering tradition of the United Empire Loyalists.

One hundred and twenty years later, much has changed. A land dispute at Caledonia, Ontario, occasioned by the construction of a housing development on lands claimed by the Six Nations, has poisoned relations between Aboriginal and non-Aboriginal residents of Grand River. As these two groups stare angrily at each other across the barricades, one can scarcely imagine two more different groups of people, two cultures apparently so separate that empathy and understanding between them seem not only lacking but impossible. History divides the contemporary residents of Grand River.

The Caledonia land dispute need not have polarized peoples who had coexisted for some two centuries. One could ask why Haudenosaunee and the citizens of Caledonia occupy the front lines, when such disputes should be settled between the Six Nations and the federal government. Unfortunately, the people living at Grand River today are the inheritors of another legacy of the eighteenth century: governments purposefully deferring issues critical to First Nations and consciously or unconsciously dividing Aboriginal and non-Aboriginal peoples. The dispute mechanism in place does not promote timely resolution of First Nations' claims. Settling with the Six Nations would encourage other First Nations to demand resolution of potentially

Above: Wall and plaque memorial to Joseph Brant outside the Mohawk Chapel, Brantford, Ontario.
Right: Brant Monument, erected in Brantford, Ontario, 1886.

hundreds of outstanding claims. With billions of dollars at stake nationwide, the government is not eager to seek justice so much as to mitigate and prolong payouts. Since the 1980s, the Six Nations alone have twenty-nine claims before the government, including one seeking compensation for the flooding of the Grand River lands by the Welland Canal Company and another involving the Grand River Navigation Company. To date, only one claim has been settled. The slowness of the process helps explain why the Haudenosaunee occupied Caledonia. The Ontario provincial government's land-use policies have compounded the problem, as the region around Grand River is slated for more intensive development, a goal that will inevitably involve more disputes over contested lands. Moreover, as frustrated First Nations, trying to push the government to resolve outstanding land claims, step up protests and road blockages, popular support for First Nations erodes. Time favours

Brant's tomb at the Mohawk Chapel, near Brantford.

the government, but more Caledonias will be the result.

Despite the vast gulf of time separating Joseph Brant's world from the present, the events of his day impinge directly on our own. Many of the participants in the Caledonia standoff descend from Natives and non-Natives who sought to create new homes on the banks of the Grand River after the Revolution. Yet, in 1784, Mohawks and Loyalists envisioned quite a different sort of community, one bound by history, common interest, and shared practices. The Brants, Hills, Youngs, and Dochsteders recreated the familiar social world of the Mohawk Valley in a modified form in order to deal with the uncertainty and newness of the Grand River.

At a time when First Nations' claims against the government promise to become both more numerous and more confrontational, it is well to think upon this more inclusive and multicultural legacy of Joseph Brant. In April 2006, Ken Young, like many Caledonia residents, manned the barricades. However, instead of joining fellow Caledonians in singing *O Canada* and hurling bread and cheese at the Six Nations in mockery of the annual distribution of presents, Young took up a position alongside the Haudenosaunee. A descendent of Loyalists who had received land from Brant, Young remembered and acted upon a now-almost-forgotten past, a past largely determined and profoundly shaped by the First Peoples.

SITES OF INTEREST

Brant Museum and Archives

A museum devoted to the cultural, social, commercial, and industrial history of Brant County and the surrounding region.
57 Charlotte Street
Brantford, ON N3T 2W6
519-752-2483
http://www.brantmuseum.ca

Canadian Museum of Civilization

This national museum devotes extensive space to First Nations' culture and history. Although not specifically related to Joseph Brant or the Six Nations, the CMC's galleries convey the diversity and complexity of Aboriginal cultures.
100 Laurier Street
Gatineau, QC K1A 0M8
819-776-7000 or 1-800-555-5621
http://www.civilization.ca/contact/contacte.html

Fort George National Historic Site

After abandoning forts in the United States in accordance with Jay's Treaty, Britain built Fort George in what is today Niagara-on-the-Lake. This site of many important councils with the Six Nations has been rebuilt and is now a living history site.
26 Queen Street
Niagara-on-the-Lake, ON L0S 1J0
905-468-4257
http://www.pc.gc.ca/lhn-nhs/on/fortgeorge/index_e.asp

Fort Klock Historic Restoration

This restored Palatine farm complex, dating to the mid-eighteenth century, is a National Historic Site. The main farmhouse was used as a fort during the American Revolution. It is now a museum and is open for tours.
Route 5
St. Johnsville, NY 13452
518-568-7779
http://fortklock.org

Grimsby Museum

This museum house dedicated to the history of the town of Grimsby (formerly Forty Mile Creek), including its Aboriginal occupation, Loyalist settlement, and subsequent growth, was the home of Robert Nelles, a Mohawk Valley Loyalist with close ties to Joseph Brant.
6 Murray Street
Box 244, Grimsby, ON L3M 4G5
905-945-5292

Indian Castle Church

Built in 1769 by William Johnson for the use of the Canajoharie Mohawks, this restored church is the only building associated with the Canajoharie Mohawks that still stands.
Route 5S
Box 172, Little Falls, NY 13365
518-823-2099
http://indiancastle.com

Iroquois Indian Museum

A museum dedicated to understanding Haudenosaunee history and culture through art. In addition to the gallery, the museum contains history exhibits.
324 Caverns Road
Howes Cave, NY 12092
518-296-8949
www.iroquoismuseum.org
info@iroquoismuseum.org

Johnson Hall

Built in 1762, Johnson Hall was the final home of Sir William Johnson. The restored museum house and grounds are open for tours.
State Historic Site
139 Hall Avenue
Johnstown, NY 12095
518-762-8712
http://www.oldfortjohnson.org

Joseph Brant Museum
The museum is a reconstruction of Brant's home at Burlington and contains a Joseph Brant exhibit hall as well as displays on other aspects of local history.
1240 North Shore Boulevard E.
Burlington, ON L7S 1C5
1-888-748-5386 or 905-634-3556
http://www.museumsofburlington.com/JBMuseum/JBMuseum.html

Mohawk Chapel
Originally called St. Paul's, this chapel is the oldest Protestant church in Ontario. The cemetery contains the graves of Joseph and John Brant.
301 Mohawk Street
Brantford, ON N3S 7V1
519-756-0240
www.mohawkchapel.ca

National Museum of the American Indian
Associated with the Smithsonian, this national museum is dedicated to telling the story of First Nations through artefact displays, artwork, and a variety of programs. Its vast collection covers a wide variety of cultures and time periods.
4th Street and Independence Avenue S.W.
Washington, DC 20560
202-633-1000
http://www.nmai.si.edu

Niagara Historical Society and Museum
A fine local museum and archive, containing numerous items belonging to Niagara Loyalists and Indian Department officers.
43 Castlereagh Street
Niagara-on-the-Lake, ON L0S 1J0
905-468-3912
www.niagarahistorical.museum

Old Fort Johnson
Sir William Johnson's second home has been restored and furnished with some of his original possessions. The museum depicts the history of both Johnson and the region.
Intersection of Routes 5 and 67
Fort Johnson, NY 12070
518-843-0300
http://www.oldfortjohnson.org

Oriskany Battlefield
This New York State Historic Site allows visitors to walk the battlefield with the assistance of interpretive signs.
7801 State Route 69
Oriskany, NY 13424
315-768-7224
http://nysparks.state.ny.us/sites/info.asp?siteID=23

Royal Ontario Museum
As one of Canada's largest museums, the ROM displays a wide selection of Aboriginal art and artefacts in its First Peoples gallery.
100 Queen's Park Crescent
Toronto, ON M5S 2C6
416-586-8000
http://www.rom.on.ca

Woodland Cultural Centre
Housed in the original Mohawk Institute Building (1828) at Grand River, this museum, art gallery, and research library focus on the Eastern Woodlands culture in general and the Six Nations in particular.
184 Mohawk Street
P.O. Box 1506
Brantford, ON N3T 5V6
519-759-2650
http://www.woodland-centre.on.ca/index.php

SELECTED BIBLIOGRAPHY

Primary Sources

Cruikshank, E.A., ed. *The Correspondence of the Honourable Peter Russell with Allied Documents Relating to His Administration of the Government of Upper Canada During the Official Term of Lieut.-Governor J. G. Simcoe.* 3 Vols. Toronto: Ontario Historical Society, 1932–1936.

———, ed. *The Correspondence of Lieut.-Governor John Graves Simcoe, with Allied Documents Relating to His Administration of the Government of Upper Canada.* 5 Vols. Toronto: Ontario Historical Society, 1925–1931.

Fernow, Berthold, comp. *New York (Colony) Council: Calendar of Council Minutes, 1668–1783.* Harrison, N.Y.: Harbor Hill Books, 1987.

Johnston, Charles M., ed. *Valley of the Six Nations: A Collection of Documents on the Indian Lands of the Grand River.* Toronto: The Champlain Society, 1964.

Norton, John. *The Journal of Major John Norton, 1816.* Edited by Carl F. Klinck and James J. Talman. Toronto: The Champlain Society, 1970.

O'Callaghan, E.B., ed. *Documents Relative to the Colonial History of the State of New York, Procured in Holland, England and France, by John R. Brodhead.* 15 Vols. Albany: Weed, Parsons, 1853–1887.

Sullivan, James, ed. *The Papers of Sir William Johnson.* 12 Vols. Albany: University of the State of New York, 1921–1965.

Secondary Sources

Anderson, Fred. *The Crucible of War: The Seven Years' War and the Fate of the Empire in British North America, 1754–1766.* New York: Alfred A. Knopf, 2000.

Axtell, James. "Dr. Wheelock's Little Red School." In Axtell, ed. *The European and the Indian: Essays in the Ethnohistory of Colonial North America.* New York and Oxford: Oxford University Press, 1981.

Carson, James T. "Molly Brant: From Clan Mother to Loyalist Chief." In Theda Perdue, ed. *Sifters: Native American Women's Lives.* New York: Oxford University Press, 2001.

Coates, Ken. "It's Time for Canada to Do Better: 150 Year-Old Debates over First Nations' Lands Has Gone on for Too Long, Prof Says," Kitchener *Record*, Oct. 30, 2006.

Elbourne, Elizabeth. "Family Politics and Anglo-Mohawk Diplomacy: The Brant Family in Imperial Context." *Journal of Colonialism and Colonial History* 6 (Winter 2005).

Feister, Lois M., and Bonnie Pulis, "Molly Brant: Her Domestic and Political Roles." In Robert S. Grumet, ed. *Northeastern Indian Lives, 1632–1816.* Amherst: University of Massachusetts Press, 1996.

Fenton, William N. *The Great Law and the Longhouse: A Political History of the Iroquois Confederacy.* Norman, Okla.: University of Oklahoma Press, 1998.

———. "Northern Iroquoian Culture Patterns." In Bruce G. Trigger, ed., *Handbook of North American Indians, Volume 15: The Northeast*. Washington, D.C.: Smithsonian Institution, 1978.

———. "Locality as a Basic Factor in the Development of Iroquois Social Structure." In William N. Fenton, ed. *Symposium on Local Diversity in Iroquois Culture.* Washington, D.C.: Government Printing Office, 1951.

Graymont, Barbara. *The Iroquois in the American Revolution*. Syracuse, N.Y.: Syracuse University Press, 1972.

Hagopian, John S. "Joseph Brant vs. Peter Russell: A Re-examination of the Six Nations' Land Transactions in the Grand River Valley." *Histoire sociale/Social History* 30 (November 1997): 300–333.

Hamilton, Milton W. *Sir William Johnson: Colonial American, 1715–1763*. Port Washington, N.Y.: Kennikat Press, 1976.

Kelsay, Isabel T. *Joseph Brant, 1743–1807: Man of Two Worlds*. Syracuse, N.Y.: University of Syracuse Press, 1986.

Knittle, Walter. *Early Eighteenth Century Palatine Emigration*. Philadelphia: Dorrance and Company, 1937.

Lydekker, John Wolfe. *The Faithful Mohawks.* Cambridge: Cambridge University Press, 1938.

Mullin, Michael J. "Personal Politics: William Johnson and the Mohawks." *American Indian Quarterly* 17 (Summer 1993): 350–58.

Nammack, Georgiana C. *Fraud, Politics, and the Dispossession of the Indians: The Iroquois Land Frontier in the Colonial Period.* Norman, Okla.: University of Oklahoma Press, 1969.

O'Donnell, James. "Joseph Brant." In R. David Edmunds, ed. *American Indian Leaders: Studies in Diversity*. Lincoln and London: University of Nebraska Press, 1980.

Otterness, Philip. *Becoming German: The 1709 Palatine Migration to New York*. Ithaca and London: Cornell University Press, 2004.

Pound, Arthur. *Johnson of the Mohawks: A Biography of Sir William Johnson, Irish Immigrant, Mohawk War Chief, American Soldier, Empire Builder*. New York: Macmillan Company, 1930.

Preston, David, "George Klock, the Canajoharie Mohawks, and the Good Ship *Sir William Johnson:* Land and Legitimacy in the Eighteenth-Century Mohawk Valley," *New York History* 86 (Fall 2005): 473–99.

Richter, Daniel K. *The Ordeal of the Longhouse: The Peoples of the Iroquois League in the Era of European Colonization*. Chapel Hill: University of North Carolina Press, 1992.

———. "Some of Them …Would Always Have a Minister with Them": Mohawk Protestantism, 1683–1719." *American Indian Quarterly* 26 (Fall 1992): 471–84.

Shannon, Timothy J. "Dressing for Success on the Mohawk Frontier: Hendrick, William Johnson, and the Indian Fashion." *William and Mary Quarterly* 3d ser., 53 (January 1996): 13–42.

———. *Indians and Colonists at the Crossroads of Empire: The Albany Congress of 1754*. Ithaca and London: Cornell University Press, 2000.

Stone, William L. *The Life of Joseph Brant —
Thayendanegea: Including the Border Wars of the American
Revolution.* 2 Vols. New York, 1838; Reprint, New York:
Kraus Reprint Co., 1969.

Taylor, Alan. *The Divided Ground: Indians, Settlers, and
the Northern Borderland of the American Revolution.* New
York: Alfred A. Knopf, 2006.

Thomas, Earle. *The Three Faces of Molly Brant.* Kingston,
Ont.: Quarry Press, 1996.

———. *Sir John Johnson, Loyalist Baronet.* Toronto and
Reading, UK: Dundurn Press, 1986.

Walkom, Thomas. "Protest Began with Potluck: Woman's
Event Marked 1784 Grant British Rewarded Loyalty with
Land." *Toronto Star.* April 22, 2006.

Weaver, Sally M. "Six Nations of the Grand River,
Ontario." In Bruce G. Trigger, ed. *Handbook of North
American Indians, Volume 15: The Northeast.* Washington,
D.C.: Smithsonian Institution, 1978.

ACKNOWLEDGEMENTS

I have incurred large debts writing this small book. The idea for the project originated with my editor, Lynn Schellenberg. Since then, she has given me scholarly independence, encouragement and a great deal of patience when I fell behind schedule. I could not have asked for more. Michel Beaulieu generously read the entire manuscript and provided equal doses of encouragement and criticism. Patricia Kennedy's careful eye made the text much better. My colleagues in the history department at Moravian College, Sandy Bardsley, Dennis Glew, Heikki Lempa, Kym Morrison, and Fran Ryan, provided a supportive and collegial atmosphere in which to work. Neither Jane Errington nor Jamey Carson had a hand in this book, but I owe them a tremendous intellectual debt. They taught me how to be a historian. I would like to acknowledge two people I have never met, Brant's major biographers, Isabel Thompson Kelsay and William Leete Stone. Although I disagree strenuously with many of their interpretations, their exhaustive research and devotion to their subject is admirable and made this book possible. The Moravian College Faculty Development and Research Committee provided generous financial support for this project through a Summer Research Stipend.

My family has always supported and encouraged my work. Many thanks to Jon, Jane, and Sue. Amelia was born about the same time this project was conceived. I am grateful she did everything in her power to keep me away from the computer. As always, Irene kept me on track. Her limitless love, patience and encouragement cannot be repaid. This book is for her.

VISUAL CREDITS

The publisher would like to thank the many archivists and librarians at the institutions supplying images for this book as well as the curators and interpretive staff at the participating sites who were so helpful in our visual acquisition. All attempts to find copyright holders have been made and any errors brought to our attention will be corrected in future editions.

The images on the following pages were photographed by Philip Scalia: 6, 12, 17, 24, 33, 34, 38, 41, 55.

The images on the following pages were photographed by Rob Skeoch at The Crawford Lake Conservation Area, The Grimsby Museum, Joseph Brant Museum, Burlington, Niagara Historical Society and Museum, Mohawk Chapel, Victoria Park, Brantford: 9L, 9R, 20M, 40TL, 44, 49R, 50T, 50M, 66M, 74, 86, 87L, 87R, 88.

Archives of Ontario: 42, 52, 64, 65, 70, 71, 76, 82; Canadian War Museum, Ottawa: 39, 45, 46; Clements Library, University of Michigan: 73; Granger Collection: 31; iStock Photo: no copyright holder: 14; Howard Rann: 40BL ; Ken Johnson, Fort Plank: 19; Johnson Hall, New York State Historic Site, Johnstown New York: 26; Johnson Hall (Sir William Johnson Presenting Medals to the Indian Chiefs of the Six Nations at Johnstown, N.Y., 1772) Edward Lamson Henry (1841-1919) 1903 oil on canvas, ht. 21 in., w. 37 in. Albany Institute of History & Art Purchase, 1993.44: 37; Library and Archives Canada: 5, 10L, 10R, 11L, 11R, 21, 22, 23M, 27T, 27BL, 28, 30, 36, 43, 47, 49M, 63, 69, 75, 77, 79, 80, 81; Library and Archives Canada, Peter Winkworth Collection of Canadiana: 48B, 67, 85T; McCord Museum: 8, 48T, 59, 78, 85B; Picture Collection, The Branch Libraries, The New York Public Library, Astor, Lenox and Tilden Foundations: 20L, 35; Ohio Historical Society: 32, 60T, 60B, 61, 62; Stewart Museum, Montreal: 23B;The Canadian Museum of Civilization: Contents page, 7, 13, 16, 18; Toronto Public Library: 15, 25L, 25R, 51, 54, 66L, 72, 83, 84; Trustees of the British Museum: Title page, 56, 57, 58.

T—top B—bottom L—left R—right

INDEX